Understanding Literacy Using Eye Movement Miscue Analysis in a Global World

Edited by Maria Perpetua Socorro U. Liwanag, Koomi J. Kim and Prisca Martens

Foreword by Eric J. Paulson

In honor and memory of

Kenneth S. Goodman (1927–2020),

our whole language teacher, mentor, friend, colleague,

and co-researcher, who taught (and continues to teach) us

to trust and respect learners, search for meaning,

ask questions, and always be learners.

Thank you, Ken! We love and miss you!

ISBN 978-1-64504-129-0 (Paperback)
ISBN 978-1-64504-130-6 (Hardback)
ISBN 978-1-64504-131-3 (E-Book)

Library of Congress Control Number: 2021944603

Printed on acid-free paper

All chapters in this book have undergone peer review
All images have been provided by individual authors

Table of Contents

Part V: Transdisciplinary EMMA Studies

List of Figures

List of Tables

Foreword

by Eric J. Paulson

If we set the beginning of Eye Movement Miscue Analysis (EMMA) research with dissertation work at the University of Arizona, we have just passed the 20-year mark of researchers combining eye movements and miscue analysis to better understand reading processes. *Understanding Literacy Using Eye Movement Miscue Analysis in a Global World* is an excellent indication of how far that approach has come—and the promise it has for going even further.

As a doctoral student at the University of Arizona in the late 1990s, I became interested in a discrepancy I saw between the findings of eye-movement research and the representation of those findings within some publications current at that time. At its most basic, some third-party summaries of the research, which were not written by the eye-movement researchers themselves, claimed that eye-movement studies supported what I viewed as reductionist, serial word-recognition models of reading. But those claims were hard to reconcile once the original eye-movement studies were examined. Plenty of work since has made it clear that eye-movement research contributes to a foundation of work that supports transactive, constructivist models.

Eye-movement research is an ecologically valid approach to capturing elements of actual, authentic reading. You can choose to ask readers to read real texts for authentic purposes, and the data that are collected do not need to be tied to tests, or remembering a reading after the fact, or doing any "non-reading" task while reading. Eye-movement data is captured unobtrusively and in situ in ways analogous to an audio recorder being used to collect speech data. And even basic eye-movement data include very detailed information on which words were fixated and which were not, variations in the number and type of words fixated, when and where regressions happen, and a range of fixation durations on different words and in different areas of the text. These data consistently provide ample evidence of the constructivist properties of reading.

I began to understand how useful eye-movement research as applied to understanding reading processes could be, and how ultimately affirming it is to researchers and instructors who understand reading as social, constructive, and process-oriented. But in terms of a more complete understanding of reading processes, it still lacked something: we could better understand what readers looked at to make sense of a text, but there is only so much information about reading processes that eye movements as a data source can provide on its own.

At about the same time that I was reading a lot of eye-movement literature, I was also learning a tremendous amount about miscue analysis, a research and evaluative approach to understanding reading that my two doctoral advisors—Ken Goodman and Yetta Goodman—created, developed, and were internationally known for. Miscues are the unexpected responses to the text that readers produce when reading aloud, and through systematic analysis of those miscues we are provided a great deal of insight into the reader's reading process and reading processes in general. This, then, is a verbal data collection process used for researching reading—and the match with eye-movement analysis seemed almost self-evident. What better pairing for a visual data collection process than a verbal data collection process? The goal then became understanding what the combination of eye-tracking methods and miscue analysis methods could teach us about readers and reading.

Using an approach that combined those research tools became my dissertation, the goal of which was to better understand the relationships between looking and reading and comprehending and texts. And per academic tradition, an acronym was born: "EMMA," for Eye Movement Miscue Analysis. Other dissertations followed, each uncovering and spotlighting new, interesting, and useful understandings about how reading works.

The approach was also picked up outside of the University of Arizona. Since 2000, EMMA research has been used by researchers in universities within and outside of the United States. These include the University of Arizona, Towson University, the University of Louisiana, Hofstra University, Wayne State University, Salisbury University, the University of Cincinnati, as well as National Taichung University in Taiwan and the University of Wollongong in Australia.

The range of research in EMMA across the years has been impressive. EMMA projects have focused on populations that include college readers, children with language impairment, elementary school students, international graduate students, bilingual elementary school students, and multilingual adult readers, among others. The research has focused on texts in several languages, multimodal reading, how readers use illustrations and images in texts, narrative texts, disciplinary texts, aspects of second-language reading, reading in different genres, reading assessments, reading music, and much more. EMMA work has contributed to theory and practice in important ways.

Which brings us back to the book at hand. One could argue that an edited book focused on a particular research methodology should cover a number of key areas: in addition to multiple stand-alone research reports, such a book should also include a sense of history of the approach, clear discussion of methods and equipment, theoretical foundations, implications for practice, and directions for the future. Understanding Literacy Using Eye Movement Miscue Analysis in a Global World does all of that, and more. The stage is first set with a review of the theoretical underpinnings of the approach to literacy that supports EMMA, and this is followed by chapters on the history and methodology of EMMA. The sections that follow include original research and scholarship on a range of literacy topics, organized into units that focus on reading process and strategy, multimodal research, and transdisciplinary studies.

The editors of the book—Maria Perpetua Socorro U. Liwanag, Koomi J. Kim, and Prisca Martens—have done outstanding work pulling together the contents of this book. There is something for everybody. And "something for everybody" may be the way to think about who will find Understanding Literacy Using Eye Movement Miscue Analysis in a Global World useful. Graduate students interested in literacy theory? Check. College professors looking for solid literacy research based on a common methodology? Check. Instructors searching for research that has clear connections to practice? Check. Researchers interested in learning more about a dynamic data collection and analysis approach? Check.

And an equally impressive lineup of scholars have authored the chapters in the book. They are a mix of both well-established and emerging researchers, writing from a multiplicity of perspectives and disciplines, based in universities on multiple continents. I am genuinely excited to see this book in print, on bookshelves, and in classrooms.

Special note here about one of those authors: Ken Goodman, to whom this book is dedicated. I still remember Ken coming to me after one of his classes, with a paper I had written for his class in his hand, saying, "This is interesting. Want to write an article about it?" Without that encouragement, I am not sure I would have understood whether some of my ideas were worth following up. Ken gave that kind of encouragement to countless students. He leaves behind such a rich legacy of literacy research and instruction that I wonder if it will ever be matched. As one of his doctoral students, I learned more from Ken than I ever thought possible, and it was my privilege and pleasure to work with him both as a student and then later as a colleague. It is fitting that the first chapter, on theory, is authored by Ken, as his work undergirds much of the research that runs throughout this book.

Eric J. Paulson
Texas State University
September 25, 2020

Introduction

by Maria Perpetua Socorro U. Liwanag, Koomi J. Kim,
and Prisca Martens

Through their transactions with all forms of texts, readers construct meaning and gain critical knowledge necessary to participate in our global society. The importance of reading in literacy makes understanding the reading process and how reading occurs critical to supporting the needs of productive citizens in our twenty-first century global society

In this book we bring together researchers nationally, internationally, and transnationally (see www.emmaforum.org), to share Eye Movement Miscue Analysis (EMMA) research that deepens and expands understandings of the reading process and addresses ways to support the literacy development of diverse populations. EMMA is an innovative method of study that combines research on eye movement and miscue analysis to examine how reading works.

In 1999 Eric Paulson and Ken Goodman combined eye movement and miscue analysis (EMMA) in their study of the reading process. Using eye tracking technology, they explored how the brain directs visual input from the eyes to guide readers' sense-making process. Although research has shown that the eyes are physiologically limited in collecting data (Paulson & Goodman, 2008), eye movement findings demonstrate how readers' perceptions extend the physical limitations of the eyes to see "more" (Goodman, Fries, & Strauss, 2016). In EMMA, researchers consider how the brain directs the eye to gather data and, through readers' miscues and retellings, what that data reveal about readers' strategies and comprehension processes.

Grounded in a comprehensive model of reading (Goodman et al., 2016; Goodman & Goodman, 2011), EMMA is an instrument for exploring the dynamic layers of complexity involved in a person's oral or silent reading. This complexity includes the reading of authentic texts (print and multimodal forms) in different genres, reading materials written in various languages, and readers from a range of ages, socio-economic statuses, and diverse cultural and linguistic backgrounds. EMMA researchers examine readers' miscues and where their eyes look to analyze readers' socio-cognitive strategies as they transact with texts, exploring how the brain uses the eyes to make sense of the text (Kim & Meyer, 2017; Liwanag, Martens, Martens, & Pelatti, 2017; Paulson, 2005).

Previous EMMA research has shown, for example, that the affordances of picturebooks influence reader strategies and comprehension (Feathers & Arya, 2015). Other studies have shown how young readers do not look at every letter or word when reading (Duckett, 2003) and that readers looked at text they omitted while focused on reading to make sense (Paulson, 2002).

The purpose of this book is to build on and further extend understandings of the reading process and diverse readers so EMMA research better supports teachers and learners around the world. The book focuses on the work of global scholars who have been influenced by the wealth of knowledge gained from studying and exploring literacies through the use of EMMA. It expands on and frames how EMMA can best be utilized to its potential to explore multiple aspects of literacies, such as reading multimodally, identifying literacy achievement, examining young children's or college readers' strategies when reading various texts, and applying EMMA in understanding varied reader strategies.

The book has five sections with chapters on a wide range of topics. These sections include a theoretical grounding in reading, background on EMMA history and methodology, and research studies related to the reading process and strategies, multimodal literacies (print and image), and transdisciplinary studies.

Part I: Theory
In his chapter Ken Goodman explains his reading model, with brain-eye functioning as a critical lens to interpret EMMA research.

Part II: History and Methodology
This section includes Yueh-Nu Hung's chapter on how two different lines of research (eye movement and miscue analysis) merged into EMMA. Poonam Arya and Maria Perpetua Socorro U. Liwanag's chapter provides an explanation of EMMA research methods.

Part III: Reading Process and Strategies
This section highlights chapters that theorize and implement EMMA as a research method and design. The chapters include varied EMMA methodologies, existing literature and implications to demonstrate what we have learned

about EMMA as a window on readers' socio-cognitive strategies and their brain-eye connections. Jessica Mantei and Lisa Kervin discuss the potential of EMMA as a research and instructional tool for examining readers' strategies during pauses as they read. Charlotte Clark, Ryan L. Nelson, Jack S. Damico, Holly L. Damico, Christine Weill, Laura E. Arrington, and Amanda Percle's chapter discusses a case study involving EMMA during shared reading with a child with special needs. Honor B. Elroy, Judith K. Franzak, Heather D. Porter, and Koomi J. Kim's work focuses on a collaborative EMMA inquiry to support a doctoral student who is learning how to understand and apply EMMA research.

Part IV: Multimodal: Print and Image

Chapters in this section examine applications of EMMA research in the larger context of the schools and communities. Poonam Arya and Karen M. Feathers' work illuminates the relationship between images and meaning-making processes of young children. Shannon Tucker and Maria Perpetua Socorro U. Liwanag discuss a case study of a second grader reading two multimodal texts. And Yueh- Nu Hung's chapter highlights insights about print and visuals in sixth grade science texts.

Part V: Transdisciplinary EMMA Studies

In this section, chapters examine multiple aspects of literacies in various professional and disciplinary fields using EMMA. The chapters also identify common themes and patterns across multiple research studies involving diverse participants of varied academic, language, and socio-cultural backgrounds and resources. Meghan East, D. Jake Follmer, and Koomi J. Kim examine college students' disciplinary literacy development using a medical laboratory science-related text. Yang Wang and Ismahan Arslan-Ari explore an international student's academic reading. And Heather Porter, Koomi J. Kim, and Judith K. Franzak focus their work on understanding a university student's disciplinary literacies using EMMA.

EMMA research plays a vital role in understanding the reading process and supporting literacy development. The findings of the studies in this book support learners, educators, and researchers in classroom (primary grades to adult settings), after school programs and other related professional fields, in a continuous exploration in understanding literacy through Eye Movement Miscue Analysis in a global world.

References

Duckett, P. (2003). Envisioning story: The eye movements of beginning readers. *Literacy Teaching and Learning, 7*(1–2), 77–89.

Feathers, K., & Arya, P. (2015). Exploring young children's use of illustrations in a picture book. *Language and Literacy, 17*(1), 42–62.

Goodman, K., Fries, P., & Strauss, S. (2016) *Reading, the grand illusion: How and why people make sense of print.* New York, NY: Routledge.

Goodman, K., & Goodman, Y. (2011). Learning to read: A comprehensive model. In R. Meyer & K. Whitmore (Eds.), *Reclaiming reading: Teachers, students, and researchers regaining spaces for thinking and action* (pp. 19–41). New York, NY: Routledge.

Kim, K., & Meyer, R. (2017). Two curricular worlds: Home and school. In R. Meyer & K. Whitmore (Eds.), *Reclaiming early childhood literacies: Narratives of hope, power, and vision* (pp. 169–179). New York, NY: Routledge.

Liwanag, M., Martens, P., Martens, R., & Pelatti, C. (2017). Examining a reader's meaning-making process with picturebooks using eye movement miscue analysis. *Literacy Research: Theory, Method, and Practice, 66*(1), 248–263.

Paulson, E. (2000). *Adult readers' eye movements during the production of oral miscues* (Doctoral dissertation). Retrieved from ProQuest Dissertations and Theses database. (UMI No. 9972086)

Paulson, E. (2005). Viewing eye movements during reading through the lens of chaos theory: How reading is like the weather. *Reading Research Quarterly, 40*(3), 338–358.

Paulson, E., & Goodman, K. (1999, January). Influential studies in eye-movement research. *Reading Online.* Retrieved from http://www.readingonline.org/research/eyemove.html.

Paulson, E., & Goodman, K. (2008). Re-reading eye-movement research: Support for transactional models of reading. In A. Flurkey, E. Paulson, and K. Goodman (Eds.), *Scientific realism in studies of reading* (pp. 25–47). New York, NY: Lawrence Earlbaum Associates.

Part I

Theory

1

Toward a Theory-Based View of Brain-Eye Functioning in Reading

What Constitutes Data and Events in Eye-Tracking Research and How the Researchers' Perspectives Influence Both

by Kenneth S. Goodman

The Eye in Reading

For well over a century, researchers have studied the movements of the eye in reading, but there is much more to reading than seeing the print (Huey, 1908; Paulson, 2005; Paulson & Goodman, 1999; Rayner & Sereno, 1994). Paul Kolers (1969) argued that reading is only incidentally visual. Reading is a dynamic activity of the human brain: a continuous process of making sense of written text.

In this chapter I argue that to understand eye-brain functions in reading, the researcher must be guided by a theoretical understanding of the process by which readers construct meaning in transactions with written texts. Eye-tracking research is a prime example of how an unexamined view of reality, and how it can and should be studied, leads to a basic misunderstanding of the functions of the brain and eye during reading. Specifically, I argue that the misuse of "the scientific method" has led to inappropriate data and a misunderstanding of what the visual and perceptual real events are in written language that need to be studied. I argue that scientific realism is a much more appropriate and productive approach to study literacy and language in general.

It is not so much that the past century of the study of eye movements in reading have produced no useful information. However, without an understanding of the whole process by which readers construct meaning, researchers have missed how much visual information is used in reading and have missed the significance of their own data.

Reading as Serial Identification of Words

To the extent that eye-tracking research has had a view of what happens in reading, researchers has assumed that reading is the serial identification of words (Adams, 1990; Rayner, 1998). This misconception leads researchers to consider that the use of the eye in reading is to send visual information to the brain to recognize words. The problem is that when eye movement research maps everything the eye is doing during reading, so many tiny pauses produced so many little data points that resembled a big Rorschach blotch. Hence, researchers decided there must be criteria for identifying what is important and what matters in all that mess. How could they crunch numbers to get a cleaner display of just what was important? From their word-oriented perspective, researchers reasoned that it would take time for the eye to stop, send an image to the cortex and then get feedback from the cortex. The best hunch was somewhere between 100 and 300 milliseconds, so researchers built into their software an algorithm that does not record anything under that threshold and the *fixation* by definition is what is considered significant.

This unit of data identified as a fixation served the purpose of cleaning up the mess, but keep in mind that the mess did not go away, it just disappeared from the analysis. The event of importance in reading became the fixation (Just & Carpenter, 1987; Paulson & Freeman, 2003).

As a result, researchers could design experiments with controlled language to get at how the eye responds to certain text conditions using this experimental method. They could create texts that were short and controlled to see how fixations differed under different conditions (Bertera & Rayner, 2000; McConkie & Rayner, 1975; Rayner, 1998; Rayner & Well, 1996).

Problems With Experimental Research

Traditional research is largely experimental. Such methodological approaches are problematic, do not address authentic reading, and disregard the complexities involved. Problems with experimental methodologies in reading research include the following principles:

(1) Experimental design requires that single aspects of the phenomenon to be studied be allowed to vary while everything else is held constant. That leads to major problems:

A. Reductionism: The researcher reduces the dynamic and complex reality of reading to small aspects. Short contrived texts designed to test hypotheses avoid the complexities of real language. The experimental reading researcher either decontextualizes what is allowed to vary or creates a minimal context stripped of the complexity of authentic reading.

B. Reification: The researcher then reifies, that is, equates this reductionism with the reality of literacy. She/he reports the study looked at the relationship between word knowledge and comprehension when in fact the study correlated two test scores of questionable face validity (face validity means, does it make any sense or does it meet qualitative criteria?).

C. Probability statistics are used to judge the strength of the finding: This requires relatively large numbers of subjects, which limits the depth of the study. The only reason for using statistical measures of probability is that more direct data aren't available for studying the phenomena. And as every statistics book points out, "garbage in, garbage out."

(2) At best, experimental research can only confirm a hypothesis—what the researcher believes to be true. It provides no new understanding of the structures and processes.

(3) Experimental research treats a dynamic process as static. The processes of reading and writing are complex and dynamic. Experimental designs turn reading into a series of discreet events. Those are not the events of authentic reading.

Conventions in a Century of Experimental Eye-Tracking Research

An early insight into how the eye functions in reading was that the eyes move from left to right along a line of print in a somewhat jerky fashion, pausing along the line at uneven intervals for variable lengths of time (Paulson & Goodman, 2008). At times the eyes regress and move back to the left. Regressions comprise ten to twenty percent of recorded eye movement fixations (Paulson, 2000; Rayner & Pollatsek, 1989).

The modern instruments used to track eye movements can be set to record fixations at various levels within the limitations of the device and the software it uses, but the algorithm is usually preset in the software provided by the manufacturer (Duchowski, 2007).

Findings from Early Experiments

Early eye movement research on reading demonstrated several key findings:

(1) There is no visual information for the brain to use during the saccade, the movement of the eye between fixations (Dodge, 1900; Paulson & Freeman, 2003; Wolverton & Zola, 1983).

(2) Only about two-thirds of words in a text receive fixations (Hogaboam, 1983; Judd & Buswell, 1922; Just & Carpenter, 1987; Paulson & Freeman, 2003; Rayner & Pollatsek, 1989).

(3) Function words are half as likely to be fixated as content words (Judd, 1918; Just & Carpenter, 1987).

In general, these findings support the view of reading as meaning construction using prediction and the selective use of cues to support the construction of meaning (though the data was not usually interpreted as showing that, particularly by secondary sources). However, they conceal the real evidence of how visual input is used in the construction of meaning.

Additionally, very few eye-tracking studies involved whole texts not written or modified for the study. Until EMMA research (Eye Movement Miscue Analysis), there were no eye-tracking studies involving analysis of miscues in oral reading which could provide insight into what the reader was comprehending.

Eye and Brain

The common algorithm for defining a fixation in reading derives from an unexamined and incorrect view of reading as sequential identification of words. It assumes that the brain responds to visual information from the eye filtered by the thalamus (labeled feedback) as each word is identified.

What We Know

Let's consider what is known (or to be more honest, what we believe we know) about how visual input from the eyes is used by the cortex of the brain where making sense of print is centered.

What we know (K. Goodman, Fries, & Strauss, 2016: Strauss, 2016):

(1) The eye is an optical instrument which has a lens that can be directed through nerve impulses to scan and focus on specific features of the visual field. The eye is continually transmitting visual impressions. These do not stop even when the eye is moving, but the cortex suppresses that input because it is fuzzy and out of focus.

(2) The light that passes through the lens turns upside down in the process. Never mind, the brain just sees it up-side up anyway. Also, there is a hole in the back of the eye, where the optical chord passes through, that gets no light. The brain just fills in where the hole would be. But we can't read in the dark (under most conditions); the eyes must have a sufficient light intensity. And as we age, the pages seem to require more light than they used to. Also, our human eyes cannot match those

of other animals (birds of prey, for example) in the area of the light spectrum we can see. If the eye is instructed to seek certain information, then it is must get directions and objectives from the cortex.

(3) The cortex is the area of the brain that makes sense of everything and, more specifically, of language. The cortex must also deal with the limitations of the eye. Making sense is a continuous ongoing process. The brain uses the senses to gather information, which it uses selectively to make sense of what it is experiencing.

Selective Use of Visual Input

The key word is *selectively*. Selective attention to the part of the visual input, while giving no attention to the rest, means that the cortex does not receive all that the eye is continuously sending and then somehow makes sense of what it sees. That would be a very slow and laborious process. Rather, the cortex suppresses much of the visual input through signals sent to the thalamus, which filters the input. The cortex then selects from the remaining visual input the information it needs to construct perceptions. The perceptions are again not simply what the cortex selects from visual input: they include what is already known or what the cortex had predicted or inferred would be seen. A perception, then is what we think we see, not what we see. All this is a part of the dynamic process of making sense. The cortex can use information from single gaze points, or any combination of them, in its construction of meaning.

Prediction

Hawkins and Blakeslee (2004) describe the cortex as an organ of prediction. The cortex is in control of the process of making sense of the text. The cortex is not a prisoner of the eye, rather it is in control of the eye, and it uses the eye to provide visual input. It directs the eye in its search for needed input. The eye does not wander aimlessly: it is efficiently looking for information (Strauss, 2016). The cortex is selective, repressing some visual input and selecting and using just what it needs to make sense of what it is doing.

Most important for reading, our eyes are limited as they focus on print to a small area around the focal point, the fovea, which is sharp and clear with diminished clarity in either direction in the parafovea and periphery. One could assume the eye bounces along evenly from fovea to fovea needing clear print all the way, but it doesn't do that. What the eye "sees" and what the cortex perceives are not the same. The brain has its focus on meaning construction, continuously predicting and sending information to the eye that controls how it directs its attention. The cortex also sends instructions to the thalamus, which suppresses some of this visual information it is receiving from the eye. In this way, it gets the information it needs without the distraction of unneeded information.

Perception

Perception is what we believe we see, and that explains why every reader produces miscues, which are mismatches between expected responses and observed responses to the text during oral reading (K. Goodman & Y. Goodman, 2014). When the oral reading appears to be "accurate," it is not because accuracy is necessary for effective reading. It is because the reader is particularly effective in making predictions and in making sense of the text. Perceptions are formed using visual information but always in the service of making sense. What we expect to see limits what we perceive. During meaning construction the brain is self-monitoring, so that if its perceptions do not make sense, that is, they do not conform to its predictions or what it has previously understood, the cortex will either reprocess the visual information it has perceived or direct the eye to regress or look again at the print to solve the problem.

Constructing Meaning (Making Sense)

Making sense is the preferred state of the brain (K. Goodman et al. 2016). During reading, the cortex is continually making sense of the text using the images from the eye, transforming visual images into perceptions. It is these perceptions which are always the result of the ongoing sense making and the visual information. The brain stores visual images, as evidenced by the times when we can't remember a name but we can "see" the face. In writing we can try several spellings to see which "looks" right.

The cortex controls the eye by setting the direction of its gaze. It makes predictions that guide the eye to seek specific information to control its focus. Because meaning making is a continuous dynamic process, a very little bit of visual input can be sufficient for the brain to confirm its predictions and make new ones. Visual input is not just useful in identifying a word—it is used in the continuous process of meaning making.

Personal Text and Published Text. Each reader constructs a personal parallel text in response to the author's published text, and that parallel text is what is comprehended (K. Goodman, 1996). This parallel text will always differ from the printed published text and from other readers' parallel texts because of what the reader brings to the reading. No two readers will ever construct the same parallel text, the same meaning.

Monitoring the Eye. Since the eye is under the control of the cortex, the cortex must be monitoring where the eye is going and what visual information it is sending. There is continuous looping between the cortex through the thalamus to and from the eye. Very small bits of visual information may be sufficient to keep the eye on track and in providing the input it is seeking. Sampling from the visual input may also explain how the cortex knows what visual information to suppress. It is evident that the eye/brain link is highly efficient needing variable amounts of visual information selectively.

Remember that the process of meaning making is dynamic and continuous. The eye and cortex are looping as selective visual input contributes to the cortex forming perceptions, and information from memory is also coming from other parts of the brain as meaning is being constructed at the speed of thought.

Distortions From an Unexamined View

Let's go back now to see how the unexamined view of reading as successive identification of words can distort what is happening in actual reading. We previously discussed that the fovea is a small area around the point where the eyes focus in a fixation. There is a larger parafovea that is "seen" but fuzzy, and again an even larger periphery where things appear shadowy. In a word-centered view, these areas are conceived as only including the part of the focal area on the line and more specifically on words on the line. However, if we drew a line around each point of fixation or gaze point, it would be more like an oval in which parts of words on the line and parts of words on lines above and below are in clear focus. Our theory indicates that the eye is seeking specific information the cortex needs, so it is entirely possible that what is selected from the visual input by the cortex is from a line above or below or from the parafovea if it matches what is predicted. Yetta Goodman and colleagues (2016) report that one fourth grader during retrospective miscue analysis explained why he corrected his miscue of *basket* for *bucket*. He said, "I knew it was a miscue because I saw *water* in the line below" (Y. Goodman, Martens, & Flurkey, 2016).

If we set our fixation parameters for shorter thresholds, we get more fixations and the foveas almost all overlap. This means that almost everything is in sharp focus at least for a short duration. So, it appears that it isn't that some parts of the print get no fixation, rather it's that the cortex is highly selective in the attention it gives to the available visual input. It may need only the briefest of gaze points, or it may need to actually have a series of longer ones close together including some to the left on previously viewed text.

In this conceptualization, the level of confidence the reader has will lead to the need for minimal spot checking to confirm all is well to considerable cautious intensive seeking of useful input. A highly confident reader will be capable of high comprehension with minimal input.

This brings into play a central concept in our view of reading: Reading is *effective* when meaning is constructed; it is *efficient* when it uses the least amount of visual input to make sense of the text (K. Goodman, 1996). In the dynamic process of making sense of written language, the same information the cortex is selecting from the visual input is used to confirm or disconfirm what has been predicted or inferred and to make new predictions. Reading is not a process of successive discrete events: it is a continuous process of meaning making.

Any gaze point or combination of gaze points may give useful information to the cortex or not. In fact, the cortex may infer information that it has not received and replace information with what was expected.

The Nature of Texts

Alan Flurkey (1997) raised questions about the concept of fluency in his dissertation. He demonstrated that all readers show considerable variation in their real time speed at different points in the text. He showed that reading doesn't flow smoothly like water through an aqueduct. The text is more analogous to a riverbed where the reader can speed up where the text is highly predictable and must slow down where the text is harder to navigate. Though highly proficient readers read more rapidly than less proficient readers, reading speed is actually more variable among highly proficient readers (Percle, Arrington, Flurkey, Damico, Weill, Damico, & Nelson, 2020).

To make sense of a text a reader must assign a grammatical structure at the beginning of each sentence. This makes it possible to predict the rest of the sentence constrained by that structure and the meaning which has already been created, and by the meaning which the reader brings to the reading of the subject of the text.

The wording of the text requires the reader to make grammatical and lexical decisions at the same time. The same visual cues are used to make all of these decisions. The reader, in fact, is constructing a text parallel to the text the author has created, and it is that text which the reader is comprehending. That means a very small amount of visual information may be all that is needed to keep the meaning making going.

Redundancy is a characteristic of texts (K. Goodman et al. 2016). Each unit of a text—whether letters, letter patterns, morphemes, words, phrases, clauses, sentences, paragraphs, and so forth—limits what can follow. How a sentence starts limits what structures it is part of. That means that any visual information at any point in the text provides information about everything subsequent. Each bit of visual information then is not discrete to the particular point in the text where it is reported to the cortex. It is part of a stream of visual information which the cortex uses to form a stream of perceptions to build an internal text which it is seeking to make sense of. At any point in the reading the cortex knows a great deal about what is likely to follow and needs very little new input to predict with some accuracy what will follow. In fact, the cortex is likely to sample from the text giving little attention to highly predictable aspects and remaining alert for unexpected input or information that is inconsistent with its predictions. The decisions the cortex sends to the eye through the thalamus always contain instructions for a possible alternative. That may not seem vital in reading but certainly is in driving a car, another situation where the instructions that are keeping the car moving at a sustained speed always must prepare the driver to respond to possible dangers without having to wait for the brain to send new instructions.

Consider also again that a focus on speed and accuracy are neither necessary nor significant in reading. Rather, we should be concerned about efficiency and effectiveness. To be effective the reader must make sense of what is read. That will never be exactly what the author was trying to convey, considering the differences between the reader and the writer. This is especially important because an "accurate rendition" is often confused with thinking reading should be accurate. Yetta Goodman (2015) stated, "accuracy in reading is not a useful goal."

Efficient reading will be relatively fast, and that is the result of efficiency. There are cases when speed would interfere with the goal of full comprehension, such as when reading texts that are difficult for the reader or when the reading is pleasing to the reader.

Let's consider fixations in the context of how visual information is used in making sense of texts. In the continuous looping between the cortex and the brain, the amount of visual information the brain needs in making sense of a text is variable depending on what we can call the density of the text and the prior knowledge the reader brings to the text (K. Goodman et al. 2016). The large number of gaze points, as short as a millisecond, indicates what may be the process of the eye sampling the text under instruction from the cortex. The brain may selectively treat much of this as background noise, or in the process of meaning construction these short gaze points or slightly longer ones may be sufficient to carry the meaning forward. However, at dense points in the text, long gaze points or close clustering of gaze points may indicate the cortex is seeking more information. That would be particularly evident when the eye is sent backward in the text for additional information or to confirm a hunch about what was missed earlier. Because there are ten times as many neurons from the cortex to the thalamus as thalamus to cortex, and because some have the function of suppressing some input, it is likely that only "just enough" visual information reaches the cortex to form perceptions. The eye continues to send data to the cortex during saccades, but the cortex may suppress such data because it would be a useless blur.

So, what, if anything, is the use of the fixation concept? Is there really a minimum necessary amount of visual input other than a single gaze point? If the eye is continuously sending visual input to the cortex, we should be more concerned with the process of selective attention. The issue is not how much visual input is sufficient, but how does the cortex select which input is useful from the continuous stream the eye is sending? Does the cortex monitor the position of the eye through attending to a series of gaze points? Can we see in the patterns of gaze points where the cortex has redirected the eye to solve a problem of loss of meaning? Would adding to our display time spent on each part of the text (Flurkey, 1997) provide a sense of variable use of visual information?

EMMA: Eye Movement Miscue Analysis

In EMMA research we add oral miscue analysis to eye tracking; that provides additional important data to use in understanding how visual information is used by the cortex (Duckett, 2008; Liwanag, Martens, Martens, & Pelatti 2017; Nelson, Damico, & Smith, 2008; O'Brien de Ramirez, 2008; Paulson, 2000, 2005). In oral reading what the cortex has constructed as a meaningful text is being represented in speech. By comparing this with the record of the eye movements we can see how efficient and effective the process has been. We can consider eye movements in what appears to be accurate reading and what the reader has changed including corrected and uncorrected miscues. Not only is this useful in our broad goal of refining our theory, is also useful in evaluating eye-tracking methodology as we try to account for what visual information was needed and used. It is rather remarkable that oral readers are always multitasking, processing the text at the same time they are expressing in speech what they have understood.

In EMMA research we can use the oral reading to consider what threshold is useful in recording gaze paths to highlight the information the reader has used. It should not be hard to play with parameters of the algorithm to consider:

- whether there is a threshold for eliminating background gaze points and what is gained and lost;
- whether the theory we are using is productive for the study of eye-brain communication;
- how our view might be useful in other eye-tracking research;
- how we can convince software and hardware designers to incorporate our theory in the design of their products.

Scientific Realism in Language Research

In scientific realism (SR) the goal of research is not to establish cause and effect (House, 1991). The goal is to develop a theory capable of discovery of the structures and processes of reality. Not to dwell on philosophy, but all forms of realism differ from idealism in that they accept the existence of the real world independent of our knowing it. The idealist considers that we may in fact construct a reality that exists only in our minds.

Scientific realism believes that the real world exists, and we can discover the structures and processes that make it what it is through scientific inquiry.

Reality can be considered at three levels (Bhaskar, 1978):

- Real
- Actual: events in which the reality shows itself
- Empirical: the view of the actual in the perspective of the researcher

Miscue analysis is based in scientific realism (SR) (K. Goodman, 2008). A miscue is an actual event: the reader has produced an observed response to the text that does not match the expected response. The SR researcher has a developing theory: miscues (observed responses) are produced in the same way as expected responses; therefore, by examining actual miscues I can get at the structures and processes of the underlying reality of reading.

An experimental researcher might empirically impose on the actual miscue the view that reading should be correct, and therefore it is an error and evidence of poor reading. In fact, most oral reading inventories do that and some even count corrections as second errors.

In the case of eye tracking, the fixation defined by an algorithm imposes on the events of eye movement a constraint on what can be considered an event worthy of consideration. It creates an artificial reality, which it substitutes for the real.

The focus of scientific realism in reading is producing a theory sufficient to explain the structures and processes of reading. What I have done here is apply the theory developed through miscue analysis to the study of eye tracking and by doing so refined the theory to get an understanding of the selective attention of the cortex to visual input in making sense of print. I also have examined the structures and processes of eye-brain communication. This chapter not only challenges misunderstandings and misconceptions of what real literacy events look like but challenges word-oriented eye-tracking methodologies. It calls for a reconsideration of eye-tracking methodologies and algorithms that mistakenly conceptualize literacy events and suggests refocusing research and associated methodologies towards the process of selective attention.

References

Adams, M. (1990). *Beginning to read: Thinking and learning about print.* Cambridge, MA: MIT Press.

Bertera, J., & Rayner, K. (2000). Eye movements and the span of the effective stimulus in visual search. *Perception and Psychophysics, 62*(3), 576–585.

Bhaskar, R. (1978). *A realist theory of science.* Hassocks, Sussex: Harvester Press.

Dodge, R. (1900). Visual perceptions during eye movement. *Psychological Review, VII,* 454–465.

Duchowski, A. (2007). *Eye tracking methodology: Theory and practice.* London: Springer.

Duckett, P. (2008). Seeing the story for the words: The eye movements of beginning readers. In A. D. Flurkey, E. J. Paulson, & K. S. Goodman (Eds.), *Scientific realism in studies of reading* (pp. 113–128). New York, NY: Lawrence Erlbaum Associates.

Flurkey, A. (1997). *Reading as flow: A linguistic alternative to fluency* (Doctoral dissertation). Available from ProQuest Dissertations and Theses database. (UMI No. 9738925)

Goodman, K. (1996). *On reading: A common-sense look at the nature of language and the science of reading.* Portsmouth, NH: Heinemann.

Goodman, K. (2008). Miscue analysis as scientific realism. In A. Flurkey, E. Paulson, & K. Goodman (Eds.), *Scientific realism in studies of reading* (pp. 7–22). New York, NY: Lawrence Erlbaum Associates.

Goodman, K., Fries, P., & Strauss, S. (2016). *Reading, the grand illusion: How and why people make sense of print.* New York, NY: Routledge.

Goodman, K., & Goodman, Y. (2014). *Making sense of learners making sense of written language: The selected works of Kenneth S. Goodman and Yetta M. Goodman.* New York, NY: Routledge.

Goodman, Y. (2015). Miscue analysis: A transformative tool for researchers, teachers, and readers. *Literacy Research: Theory, Method and Practice. 64*(1), 92–111.

Goodman, Y., Martens, P., & Flurkey, A. (2016). Revaluing readers: Learning from Zachary. *Language Arts, 93*(3), pp. 213–225.

Hawkins, J., & Blakeslee, S. (2004). *On intelligence.* New York, NY: Times Books.

Hogaboam, T. (1983). Reading patterns in eye movement data. In K. Rayner (Ed.), *Eye movements in reading* (pp. 309–332). New York, NY: Academic Press.

House, R. (1991). Realism in research. *Educational Researcher, 20*(6), pp. 2–9.

Huey, E. (1908). *The psychology and pedagogy of reading.* Cambridge, MA: MIT Press.

Judd, C. (1918). *Reading: Its nature and development.* Chicago, IL: University of Chicago Press.

Judd, C., & Buswell, G. (1922). *Silent reading: A study of the various types.* Chicago, IL: University of Chicago Press.

Just, M., & Carpenter, P. (1987). *The psychology of reading and language comprehension.* Newton, MA: Allyn and Bacon.

Kolers, P. (1969). Reading is only incidentally visual. In K. Goodman & J. Fleming (Eds.), *Psycholinguistics and the teaching of reading.* Selected papers from the IRA Pre-Convention Institute held in Boston, April 1968 (pp. 8–16). Newark, DE: International Reading Association.

Liwanag, M., Martens, P., Martens, R., & Pelatti, C. (2017). Supporting multilingual learners as readers: Lessons from eye movement miscue analysis. *English Journal, 106*(3), 79–82.

McConkie, G., & Rayner, K. (1975). The span of the effective stimulus during a fixation in reading. *Perceptions and Psychophysics, 17,* 578–586.

O'Brien de Ramirez, K. (2008). *Silent, oral, L1, L2, French and English reading through eye movements and miscues* (Doctoral dissertation). Retrieved from ProQuest Dissertations and Theses database. (UMI No. 3336609)

Paulson, E. (2000). *Adult readers' eye movements during the production of oral miscues* (Doctoral dissertation). Retrieved from ProQuest Dissertations and Theses database. (UMI No. 9972086)

Paulson, E. (2005). Viewing eye movements during reading through the lens of Chaos Theory: How reading is like the weather. *Reading Research Quarterly, 40*(3), 338–358.

Paulson, E., & Freeman, A. (2003). *Insight from the eyes: The science of effective reading instruction.* Portsmouth, NH: Heinemann.

Paulson, E., & Goodman, K. (1999, January). Influential studies in eye-movement research. *Reading Online* (Retrieved November 20, 2016), from http://www.readingonline.org/research/eyemove.html.

Paulson, E., & Goodman, K. (2008). Re-reading eye-movement research: Support for transactional models of reading. In A. Flurkey, E. Paulson, and K. Goodman (Eds.), *Scientific realism in studies of reading* (pp. 25–47). New York, NY: Lawrence Earlbaum Associates.

Percle, A., Arrington, L., Flurkey, A., Damico, H., Weill, C., Damico, J., & Nelson, R. (2020). Illuminating the complexity of oral reading fluency: A multiple lens approach. *Literacy Research: Theory, Method, and Practice, 69*(1), 358-376..

Nelson, R., Damico, J., & Smith, S. (2008). Applying eye movement miscue analysis to the   reading patterns of children with language impairment. *Clinical Linguistics and Phonetics, 22*(4–5), 293–303.

Rayner, K. (1998). Eye movements in reading and information processing: 20 years of research. *Psychological Bulletin, 124*(3), 372–422.

Rayner, K., & Pollatsek, A. (1989). *The psychology of reading.* Hillsdale, NJ: Lawrence Erlbaum Associates.

Rayner, K., & Sereno, S. (1994). Eye movement in reading: Psycholinguistic studies. In M. A. Gernsbacher (Ed.), *Handbook of psycholinguistics* (pp. 57–81). San Diego, CA: Academic Press.

Rayner, K., & Well, A. (1996). Effects of contextual constraint on eye movement in reading: A further examination. *Psychonomic Bulletin and Review, 3,* 504–509.

Strauss, S. (2016). Discussion of a model on human consciousness. In G. Leisman & J. Merrick (Eds.), *Considering consciousness clinically* (pp. 217–232). Hauppauge, NY: Nova Science.

Wolverton, G., & Zola, D. (1983). The temporal characteristics of visual information extraction during reading. In K. Rayner (Ed.), *Eye movements in reading* (pp. 41–51). New York, NY: Academic Press.

Part II

History and Methodology

2

History of Eye Movement Miscue Analysis (EMMA)

by Yueh-Nu Hung

History of Eye Movement Research

The studies of the eyes and eye movements can be traced back more than 2000 years to Aristotle, who noted the binocular feature of eye movements (Wade, 2010). According to Wade (2010), eye movement research is generally considered to have originated in the nineteenth century. The French ophthalmologist Louise Emile Javal, who is the first person to use the word "saccade" to refer to the jerky movements between fixations, is considered the founder of eye movement research because of American psychologist Huey's citation of Javal's work in his seminal book on the psychology of reading (Huey, 1908).

At around the turn of the century, eye trackers were designed and built to record the movements of the eyes. Orschansky's (1899) apparatus used a mirror attached to an aluminum eye-cup. It recorded the light on the mirror reflected from the surface of the eye due to movements (cited in Wade and Tatler, 2005). Later designs of eye-tracking devices were not as unpleasant for the reader as the earlier models. Guy Thomas Buswell from the University of Chicago invented the first non-intrusive eye tracker in 1920 (Buswell, 1922). Models of eye trackers continued to be more user-friendly and affordable as well. The remote models of eye trackers did not require the reader to put on or wear anything on the head. The easiness and effortlessness of eye tracking ushered in a large amount of eye movement research in the 1980s and 1990s.

The pioneers of the study of the eyes focused on the anatomy, the binocularity, and the voluntary and involuntary movements of the eye. In the 1950s and 1960s scholars began to understand the connection between eye movements and attention. In a classic study conducted by Yarbus (1967/1990), the painting *The Unexpected Visitor* by Ilya Repin was shown seven times to an

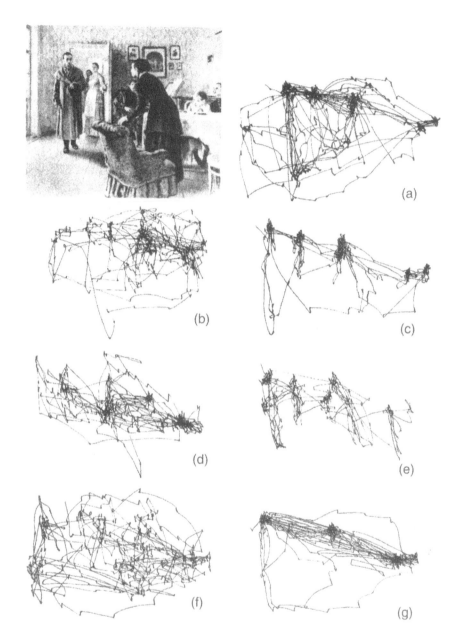

Figure 2.1: Eye Movement Record From Yarbus's Classic Study (1967, p. 174)

Note: The seven purposes of reading were (a) free examination; (b) estimate the material circumstances of the family in the picture; (c) give the ages of the people; (d) surmise what the family had been doing before the arrival of the "unexpected visitor"; (e) remember the clothes worn by the people; (f) remember the position of the people and objects in the room; and (g) estimate how long the "unexpected visitor" had been away from the family. Reprinted from Springer and Plenum Press. *Eye movements and vision* (B. Haigh, Trans.), 1967. Yarbus, A., L. with permission from Springer Science+Business Media, LLC.

observer but each time different instructions were given, such as "Guess the ages of the people in the picture," "Remember the clothes worn by the people," and "Guess what the people were doing before the arrival of the unexpected visitor." Eye movement data showed that higher order factors such as purpose and attention guided the movements of the eyes (see Figure 2.1). Yarbus wrote that "Eye movements reflect the human thought processes; so the observer's thought may be followed to some extent from records of eye movement" (Yarbus, 1967/1990, p. 190).

In his review of eye movements and reading, O'Regan (1990) indicated that earlier eye movement research in reading was conducted with a view to understand the underlying perceptual process. Starting from around the 1980s, because of interest in linguistics and psycholinguistics, researchers used "eye movements as an indicator of the reader's cognitive processes" (p. 395). Conklin, Pellicer-Sánchez, and Carrol (2018) also pointed out that the driving force behind the rise in eye movement research in the 1980s was the belief that there was a close connection between eye movements and cognitive processing. The eye-mind hypothesis, proposed by Just and Carpenter (1980, 1984), stated that what was being looked at by the eyes was being processed by the mind (brain). Conklin et al. (2018) wrote that "tracking eye-movements provides a window into a largely unconscious behavior" (p. 2).

The long history of eye movement research has yielded a solid knowledge base about eye movements in reading. Measures of eye movements examine reading and viewing performances. Castelhano and Rayner (2008) and Rayner (1995, 1998, 2009) report that for adults who read their first language fluently, the mean fixation duration is around 225–250 ms in silent reading and 297–325 in oral reading. Mean saccade size is two visual degrees (about 7–9 letter spaces) in silent reading and 1.5 visual degrees (about 6–7 letter spaces) in oral reading. These are global measures of eye movements. In each reading or viewing event, eye movements are reflective of various reader, textual, and contextual influences. Eye-tracking technology has been used in a wide range of disciplines such as medical education, advertising, visual and graphic design, web viewing, and human-computer interaction. Reading research, however, has had the most eye movement research.

History of Miscue Analysis Research

Like eye movement research, miscue analysis research also has a long history that dates back to the 1960s. Rooted in Ken Goodman's sociocultural psycholinguistic view of reading, miscue analysis provides an alternative to the evaluation of reading performance and the reader. "Miscues" are the differences between the expected reading (what is written) and the observed reading (what is actually read aloud). Such differences are traditionally considered to be errors or mistakes on the part of the reader because of lack of reading proficiency or carelessness. In miscue analysis, however, teachers/researchers believe that the same reading process and strategies explain when readers miscue and when they don't. Miscues are never random. Readers who miscue use linguistic cues from the text and apply comprehension strategies like proficient readers do but in a less effective or efficient way (Brown, Goodman, & Marek, 1996; Y. Goodman, 1995). Miscues are mis-uses of language cues, and they provide a "window on the reading process" (Goodman, 1973, p. 5).

Figure 2.2 below shows miscues made by a 10-year-old English language learner whose native language was Mandarin Chinese. The original text read, "He comes out at night and eats little frog children for supper." The reader read, "He comes out at the night and eat little frog children for super." The first miscue was the insertion "the" between "at" and "night." The second miscue was the substitution of "eat" for "eats." And the third miscue was the substitution of "super" for "supper." While "super" and "supper" are graphophonically similar (they look and sound similar), "super" makes the sentence syntactically (grammatically) and semantically (meaning) unacceptable. The reader did not correct these three miscues, indicating his still developing command of English.

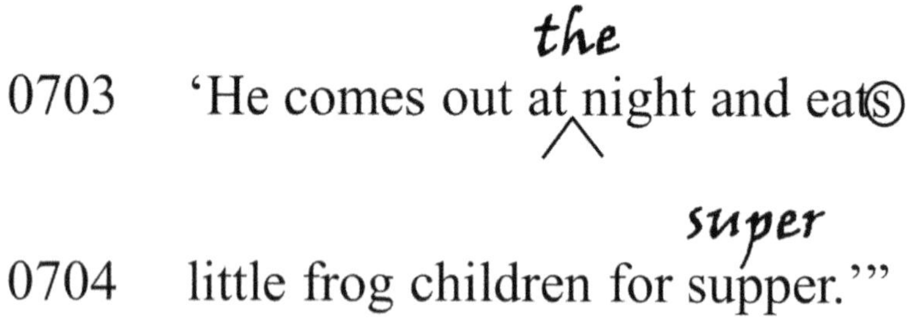

the
0703   'He comes out at night and eats

super
0704   little frog children for supper.'"

Figure 2.2: Examples of Miscues
Source: Author.
Source: Lobel, A. (1979, p. 7). "Shivers" in *Days with Frog and Toad*. New York: HarperTrophy.

However, later in the story where it reads, "Then I saw two huge eyes," the reader read, "Then I saw two big eyes" (see Figure 2.3). In this substitution miscue, the same reader showed good control of the syntactic and semantic structures of the sentence. The prediction for what might follow "two" was so strong that the graphophonic information of "huge" was overridden in part. Both "huge" and "big" contain the letter "g," though the sounds are different (graphophonic), both are adjectives (syntactic), and both have similar meanings (semantic), making the sentence syntactically and semantically acceptable. These examples show how miscues reveal linguistic and meaning processing in reading and the difficulties and strengths of the reader in the reading process.

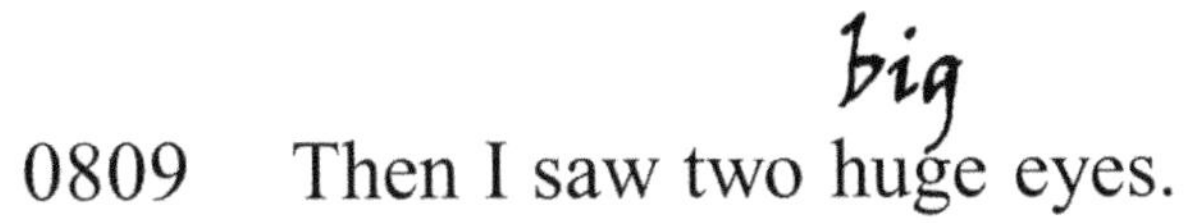

0809   Then I saw two huge eyes.

big

Figure 2.3: An Example of a Miscue
Source: Author.
Source: Lobel, A. (1979, p. 8). "Shivers" in *Days with Frog and Toad*. New York: HarperTrophy.

Goodman's concept of tentative information processing and reading miscues was first published in 1967 in a classical article titled "Reading: A Psycholinguistic Guessing Game" (Goodman, 1967). His sociocultural transactional psycholinguistic theories of reading upon which miscue analysis research is based are fully explicated in his book *On Reading* (1996) and book chapter "Reading, Writing and Written Language: A Sociopsycholinguistic Transactional View" (Goodman, 1994). Goodman's colleagues have made miscue analysis available for classroom teachers by developing classroom procedures and resources to support the use of miscue analysis as an alternative to traditional paper and pencil tests (Goodman, Watson, & Burke, 1987, 2005).

Since the 1960s, Ken Goodman and his colleagues have been using miscue analysis to research reading comprehension processes, the readers' comprehension strengths, difficulties and strategies, and text factors that influence reading. Miscue analysis has been especially valued as a tool to understand not just the result of reading (that is, comprehension) but also the process of reading (comprehending, in Goodman's term). Miscue analysis reveals how readers orchestrate various sound, spelling, syntactic, semantic, and contextual information to make sense of written language.

In 1982 Ken Goodman (2003) introduced the concept of revaluing, and by the 1990s he and his colleagues were inviting readers to listen to recordings of their own or others' oral readings and discuss retrospectively what might have caused the miscues. These conversations helped readers become metacognitively aware of their own reading processes and their strengths and difficulties. The discussions about the miscues, sound and spelling similarity, and syntactic and semantic acceptability have also helped readers to become more metalinguistically aware of the written language (Y. Goodman & Marek, 1996). Retrospective Miscue Analysis (RMA) is a powerful tool to help readers "revalue" themselves and see themselves as active readers using different types of language cues to construct meaning (Y. Goodman, 1996; Y. Goodman, Martens, & Flurkey, 2014; Martens, 1998).

History of EMMA

The idea of examining the reader's eye movements together with the analysis of oral miscues was originally suggested by Gollasch (1980). The idea was not put into practice, though, until around the turn of the century at the University of Arizona when Eric Paulson came to study with Ken Goodman. Paulson's doctoral dissertation *Adult Readers' Eye Movements during the Production of Oral Miscues*, completed in 2000, was the first attempt to combine eye movement and miscue analysis research methods to investigate reading processes. Paulson created the acronym EMMA (eye movement miscue analysis) to refer to this new line of reading research. He wrote:

> Miscue analysis, the psycholinguistic analysis of unexpected responses in a reader's oral text, provides a verbal dimension of data for reading research. Similarly, eye-movement recording, which shows precisely where in a text a reader looks, provides a visual dimension of data. When these two research approaches are combined, both verbal and visual data are analyzed, resulting in a powerful, multi-dimensional view of the reading process. (Paulson, 2000, p. 18)

Earlier eye movement research that involved oral reading or reading errors was more concerned with eye movement performances relative to the existence of reading errors, not the nature of errors or reading process (Paulson, 2000). EMMA research, however, juxtaposed eye movement information and reading miscue information to increase the depth and width of the window into the reading processes. In this seminal study, Paulson was able to show that most miscued words were fixated before the miscue was made, which is contrary to the traditional wisdom believing that reading miscues resulted from laziness or carelessness on the part of the reader.

In the earlier example of the 10-year-old English learner's miscues (Figures 2.2 & 2.3), the eye movement information makes visible what the learner was seeing at the moment he produced the miscues. In the substitution miscue of "super" for "supper" (see Figure 2.4), he did not skip or ignore "supper." On the contrary, he made a total of five fixations on it (circles in the figure indicate fixations). He also made a total of four fixations on "at night," which he read "at the night" with an insertion of "the," and one fixation on "eats" that he read "eat." These examples clearly illustrate this English learner's effort at using graphophonic and syntactic cues to make sense of a language he was still learning.

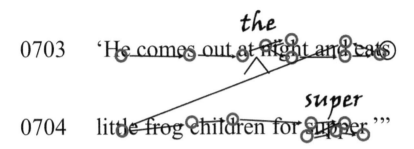

Figure 2.4: Eye Fixations on Text

Note: When eye fixations are overlaid on the miscues and the reading text, greater information is revealed about the reader's visual attention and attempts at meaning processing. The line shows the saccades [eye movements between fixations (circles)].
Source: Author.
Source: Lobel, A. (1979, p. 7). "Shivers" in *Days with Frog and Toad*. New York: HarperTrophy.

Based on the work of Paulson and his colleagues (Duckett, 2003; Paulson and Freeman, 2003), many EMMA studies have been conducted to explore a variety of reading research topics. In a short review of EMMA research, Hung (2019) points out that EMMA research method has been often used to understand the reading of picture books. The eye-tracking part of the method makes it possible to learn where the reader is looking on the illustrated text. Liwanag, P. Martens, R. Martens, and Pelatti have explored this in several EMMA studies (Liwanag, Martens, Martens, & Pelatti, 2017; Liwanag, Pelatti, Martens, & Martens, 2016). EMMA has also been used to investigate the reading of science text (Hung, 2014; Hung, Kuo, & Liao, 2019) and how children use visual information and different language cues to assist comprehension (Arya & Feathers, 2012; Feathers & Arya, 2015). In response to a call by Gollasch (1980), Hung (2019) conducted an EMMA study to understand the complex processes of reading an authentic text with intentionally embedded errors. The combination of the oral miscue and the eye movement data revealed what readers saw, what they read aloud, and what they possibly thought.

In *Reading, the Grand Illusion* (Goodman, Fries, & Strauss, 2016), Goodman and his colleagues provide a robust theoretical foundation to support the use of EMMA in reading research. The authors believe that EMMA research provides good evidence to support a constructivist view of reading.

Looking Back and Looking Forward

Eye movement research has a longer history than that of miscue analysis research. Eye tracking and eye movements were first added to the analysis of miscues to understand how and why miscues happen and where the reader was looking when a miscue was made. In an interview with Eric Paulson, he said that what EMMA showed him about reading was "the power of the reader and the readers' expectations and predictions and knowledge, cultural knowledge, social knowledge, cognitive, technical knowledge, knowledge about the text, knowledge about the content area, and how that knowledge can overpower the print information that's there" (Personal communication, December 11, 2019). EMMA research reveals that when reading, the brain controls the eyes. The brain uses the visual information collected and sent by the eyes to construct a text.

For the future of EMMA, there are three suggested directions. First, EMMA can be used as a research method to explore more issues on reading and comprehension. For example, how different text factors (genre, difficulty, language style, etc.) and reader factors (age, proficiency, first vs. second language, content knowledge, purpose, etc.) influence comprehension. Second, EMMA research can be used to promote understandings about reading. Findings of EMMA research can be shared with classroom teachers and even with parents to help them understand the reading process and how to better support their children as readers.

Finally, EMMA can be used as an approach, instead of a set of fixed procedures, in reading research. In recognition of the ever increasing multi-modal and non-linear nature of reading, it is important to know how readers make use of not just linguistic cues (such as graphophonic, syntactic, and semantic language cues) but also the non-linguistic cues (illustrations, text features, print-text relations, etc.). To make the reading task in EMMA research even more authentic, instead of asking readers to read aloud print, researchers can encourage them to read and view the text in ways they want. Eye movement information (such as regressions, number of words with no or multiple fixations, and duration of fixations) combined with reader's retrospective reflections can inform the reading process as the analysis of miscues does. As Paulson stated, if EMMA is used as an approach, then there is "a ton of work that we can do and better understand how readers read texts of all types" (Personal communication, December 11, 2019).

References

Arya, P., & Feathers, K. M. (2012). Reconsidering children's readings: Insights into the reading process. *Reading Psychology, 33*(4), 301–322.

Brown, J., Goodman, K. S., & Marek, A. M. (1996). *Studies in miscue analysis: An annotated bibliography.* Newark, DE: International Reading Association.

Buswell, G. T. (1922). *Fundamental reading habits: A study of their development.* Chicago, IL: University of Chicago Press.

Castelhano, M. S., & Rayner, K. (2008). Eye movements during reading, visual search, and scene perception: An overview. In K. Rayner, D. Shen, X. Bai & G. Yan (Eds.), *Cognitive and cultural influences on eye movements* (pp. 3–33). Tianjin, China: Tianjin People's Publishing House.

Conklin, K., Pellicer-Sánchez, A., & Carrol, G. (2018). *Eye-tracking: A guide for applied linguistics research.* Cambridge: Cambridge University Press.

Duckett, P. (2003). Envisioning story: The eye movements of beginning readers. *Literacy Teaching and Learning, 7*(1–2), 77–89.

Feathers, K. M., & Arya, P. (2015). Exploring young children's patterns of image use in a picturebook. *Language and Literacy, 17*(1), 42–62.

Gollasch, F. V. (1980). *Readers' perception in detecting and processing embedded errors in meaningful text* (Unpublished doctoral dissertation). University of Arizona, Tucson, Arizona.

Goodman, K. S. (1967). Reading: A psycholinguistic guessing game. *Journal of the Reading Specialist, 6*(4), 126–135.

Goodman, K. S. (1973). Miscues: Windows on the reading process. In K. S. Goodman (Ed.), *Miscue analysis: Applications to reading instruction* (pp. 3–14). Urbana, IL: ERIC Clearinghouse on Reading and Communication Skills and the National Council of Teachers of English.

Goodman, K. S. (1996). *On reading.* Plymouth, NH: Heinemann.

Goodman, K. S. (1994). Reading, writing, and written texts: A transactional sociopsycholinguistic view. In R. B. Ruddell, M. R. Ruddell & H. Singer (Eds.), *Theoretical models and processes of reading* (4th ed., pp. 1093–1130). Newark, DE: International Reading Association.

Goodman, K. S. (2003). Revaluing readers and reading. In A. Flurkey & J. Xu (Eds.), *On the revolution of reading: The selected writings of Kenneth S. Goodman* (pp. 421–429). Portsmouth, NH: Heinemann.

Goodman, K. S., Fries, P. H., & Strauss, S. L. (2016). *Reading, the grand illusion.* New York, NY: Routledge.

Goodman, Y. M. (1995). Miscue analysis for classroom teachers: Some history and some procedure. *Primary Voices K–6, 3*(4), 2–9.

Goodman, Y. M. (1996). Revaluing readers while readers revalue themselves: Retrospective miscue analysis. *The Reading Teacher, 49*(8), 600–609.

Goodman, Y., Martens, P., & Flurkey, A. (2014). *The essential RMA: A window into reader's thinking.* Katonah, NY: Richard C. Owen.

Goodman, Y., & Marek, A. (1996). *Retrospective miscue analysis: Revaluing readers and reading.* Katonah, NY: Richard C. Owen.

Goodman, Y. M., Watson, D. J., & Burke, C. L. (1987). *Reading miscue inventory: Alternative procedures.* Katonah, NY: Richard C. Owen.

Goodman, Y. M., Watson, D. J. & Burke, C. L. (2005). *Reading miscue inventory: From evaluation to instruction* (2nd ed.). Katonah, NY: Richard C. Owen.

Huey, E. B. (1908). *The psychology and pedagogy of reading.* New York: Macmillan.

Hung, Y.-N. (2014). What are you looking at? An eye movement exploration in science text reading. *International Journal of Science and Mathematics Education, 12*(2), 241–260.

Hung, Y.-N. (2019). Fifth grade students reading a Chinese text with embedded errors: An eye movement miscue analysis study. *Reading Psychology, 40*, 397–424.

Hung, Y.-N., Kuo, H.-Y., & Liao, S.-C. (2019). Seeing what they see: Elementary EFL students reading science texts. *RELC Journal.* DOI: 10.1177/0033688219854475

Just, M. A., & Carpenter, P. A. (1980). A theory of reading: From eye fixations to comprehension. *Psychological Review, 87*(4), 329–354.

Just, M. A., & Carpenter, P. A. (1984). Using eye fixations to study reading comprehension. In D. E. Kieras & M. A. Just (Eds.), *New methods in reading comprehension research* (pp. 151–182). Hillsdale, NJ: Lawrence Erlbaum Associates.

Liwanag, M. P. S. U., Martens, P., Martens, R., & Pelatti, C. Y. (2017). Examining a reader's meaning-making process of picture books using eye movement miscue analysis. *Literacy Research: Theory, Method, and Practice, 66*(1), 248–263.

Liwanag, M. P. S. U., Pelatti, C. Y., Martens, R., & Martens, P. (2016). Children's eye movements, miscue analysis patterns, and retellings when reading a counterpoint picture book. *Literacy Research: Theory, Method, and Practice, 65*(1), 253-267.

Land, M. F., & Tatler, B. W. (2009). *Looking and acting: Vision and eye movements in natural behaviour.* Oxford and New York: Oxford University Press.

Lobel, A. (1979). *Days with Frog and Toad.* New York: HarperTrophy.

Martens, P. (1998). Using retrospective miscue analysis to inquire: Learning from Michael. *The Reading Teacher, 52*(2), 176–180.

O'Regan, J. K. (1990). Eye movements and reading. In E. Kowler (Ed.), *Eye movements and their role in visual and cognitive processes* (pp. 395–453). Amsterdam & New York: Elsevier.

Orschansky, J. (1899). Eine Methode die Augenbewegungen direct zu untersuchen. *Centralblatt für Physiologie, 12*, 785–790.

Paulson, E. J. (2000). *Adult readers' eye movements during the production of oral miscues* (Unpublished doctoral dissertation). University of Arizona, Tucson, AZ.

Paulson, E. J., & Freeman, A. E. (2003). *Insight from the eyes: The science of effective reading instruction.* Portsmouth, NH: Heinemann.

Rayner, K. (1995). Eye movements and cognitive processes in reading, visual search, and scene perception. In J. M. Findlay, R. Walker & R. W. Kentridge (Eds.), *Eye movement research: Mechanisms, processes, and applications* (pp. 3–21). New York: Elsevier Science.

Rayner, K. (1998). Eye movements in reading and information processing: 20 years of research. *Psychological Bulletin, 124*(3), 372–422.

Rayner, K. (2009). Eye movements and attention in reading, scene perception, and visual research. *Quarterly Journal of Experimental Psychology, 62*(8), 1457–506.

Wade, N. J. (2010). Pioneers of eye movement research. *i-Perception, 1*(2), 33–68.

Wade, N. J., & Tatler, B. W. (2005). *The moving tablet of the eye: The origins of modern eye movement research.* New York: Oxford University Press.

Yarbus, A. L. (1967/1990). *Eye movements and vision* (B. Haigh, Trans.). New York, NY: Plenum.

3

Eye Movement Miscue Analysis (EMMA) Methodology

by Poonam Arya and Maria Perpetua Socorro U. Liwanag

The past 20 years have brought numerous changes in eye-tracking machines, resulting in changes in the design of eye movement miscue analysis (EMMA) studies. What has remained consistent with EMMA as a research methodology is the view of reading as a transactional socio-psycholinguistic process. Through EMMA, researchers document how the brain and the eyes are heuristic tools for understanding the ways in which we construct meaning when reading (Goodman, Fries, & Strauss, 2016).

Research on eye tracking over several decades has produced valuable information about what the eyes do when reading (e.g., Ehrlich & Rayner, 1981; Inhoff, Pollatsek, Possner, & Rayner, 1989; Rayner, 2009). Further, a great deal has been learned about the reading process through an examination of the relationship between what the eyes look at and what readers say when they read orally (Arya & Feathers, 2012; Duckett, 2002; Hung, 2019; Liwanag, P. Martens, R. Martens, & Pelatti, 2017; Nelson, Damico, & Smith, 2008; Paulson, 2005; Paulson & Freeman, 2003; Porter, Kim, Franzak, & MacDonald, 2020).

In this chapter, we review the tools and methodologies utilized by researchers since miscue analysis procedure first merged with eye-tracking methods to create EMMA. We also discuss future avenues for research that this methodology offers.

Eye Movement Miscue Analysis Tools

To understand how eye movements and miscue analysis data help illuminate what we know about the reading process, in this section we examine how data is collected when using an eye-tracking machine in combination with miscue analysis. Specifically, we explain the tools and methods used along with the collected eye movement and miscue analysis (Goodman, Watson, & Burke, 2005) measures that allow the researchers to better understand the relationship between the measures and the overall reading process.

Eye-Tracking Methods

We study readers' eye movements and the reading process through the use of various eye-tracking machines. With each eye-tracking machine comes an array of stand-alone or built-in software from numerous manufacturers that allow researchers to design and build experiments, collect eye movement measures, and analyze collected eye movement measures based on the researchers' specifications. A growing number of eye-tracking machines have been available in the market, and some of the eye trackers utilized by EMMA researchers are Applied Science Laboratories Desktop Models 504, D6, D7-Eye Trackers and Mobile Eye, EyeLink Portable Duo and EyeLink 1000 plus by SR Research, iView ETG portable by SMI, and Tobii Pro X3-120. Additional information about the hardware and associated software is listed in Appendix A.

The goal of eye movement measurement and analysis is to gain insight into a reader's attentive behavior. This methodology is based on the "eye-mind" concept (Just & Carpenter, 1980) which suggests that eye movements provide dynamic information of where a reader is focusing attention. Prior to the 1990s, a reader's head was held in place by bite bars, chin rests, headrests, and other devices so that only the eyes moved. Then a beam of light reflecting off the cornea was used to track eye movements. In recent years, advanced computers and increased sophistication in eye tracking (e.g., use of head trackers) has made tracking of eye movements both reliable and comfortable and allowed researchers to use varied text displays to understand the reading process.

The fields of neuroscience and psychology have greatly influenced the methods used in eye-tracking research. Neuroscientists have studied "the cognitive and behavioral aspects of vision . . . which present frameworks for understanding human saccadic eye movement" (Duchowski, 2002, p. 455). Additionally, researchers have used functional brain imaging along with eye movements to study the cortical activity that is related to a subject's attentional mechanisms, such as fixations and saccades (Özyurt, DeSouza, West, Rutschmann, & Greenlee, 2001). Although we know that the brain continuously learns from the environment, eye movement research shows that there is a lull in this continuous input when the eyes are moving from one spot to another (Liversedge, Gilchrist, & Everling, 2011). During this saccadic movement, "it is considered safe to say that we are blind" (Holmqvist, Nystrom, Anderson, Dewhurst,

Jarodzka, & van de Weijer, 2015, p. 23). However, when the eye stops, it "focuses on the text in order for that part of the text to be useful for the reader" (K. Goodman et al., 2016, p. 20). The in-focus region is called the fovea, and even though readers are able to physiologically discern this foveal region, "letters that are viewed outside of that window are seen as gross shapes, not as distinguishable, in-focus letters" (K. Goodman et al., 2016, p. 20).

Eye-tracking research in reading and other information-processing tasks done by psychologists further inform our methodological understandings (e.g., Rayner, 1998; Reichle, Pollatsek, Fisher, & Rayner, 1998). Most of the studies are descriptive in nature where the location and times of a readers' eye movements are recorded during the reading of text (Buswell, 1936; Huey, 1900). In addition, "three experimental paradigms, the moving window, the boundary, and the foveal mask" (Duchowski, 2002, p. 457) have been used to study eye movements. In the gaze-contingent moving window paradigm (McConkie & Rayner, 1975), a variable rectangular window is created around a fixated word to control the amount of information available to the reader. That is, the text appears normal within a window of a certain character length, but beyond that the text is garbled. Eye movements are recorded as the subject reads with windows of various sizes to determine the window size that matches the reading when there is no window, thereby providing an accurate estimate of the perceptual scan. This technique has pointed out that for readers of English, the perceptual span is very limited; three to four letters to the left of fixation and 14–15 letters to the right of fixation (Rayner & Bertera, 1979, as cited in Rayner, Slattery, & Belanger, 2010).

In the boundary technique (Rayner, 1975), the researcher selects a predefined marker or boundary before a target word, and as the readers' eyes cross the invisible boundary (e.g., end of a line), the stimulus displayed to the reader is replaced by the target word. This technique allows the researcher to examine the kind of information a reader extracts when the target word is in the parafoveal vision. In the foveal mask technique (Rayner & Bertera, 1979), a string of letters or X's are used to cover the target word, and the reader is either presented with a parafoveal view that is identical to the target word or a variation of the target word (usually an orthographically similar nonword). This allows the researchers to study the impact of parafoveal preprocessing by analyzing the difference in gaze durations on the target word depending on the type of parafoveal mask used.

Some of the commonly used eye movement measures include number of fixations, fixation duration, regressions, and transitions (see Figure 3.1). These and other measures are defined below.

- Fixation: When a reader holds the central foveal vision in place (maintains their visual gaze on a single spot of a displayed stimulus)

- Fixation Duration: Amount of time a reader spends looking at a particular spot of a displayed stimulus

- Regression: When a reader returns their gaze to a particular spot of a displayed stimulus (for English texts, a movement from right to left or bottom to top)

- Saccade: When a reader moves the fovea rapidly from one point of interest to another on a displayed stimulus; no useful visual information is acquired during a saccade.

- Transition: Eye movement between different parts of a displayed stimulus (e.g., text to image, image to text, image to image)

- Visual Span: How many words a reader can read before and after the currently fixated word

- Area of interest (AOI): A tool to select regions of a displayed stimulus to extract metrics specifically for those regions

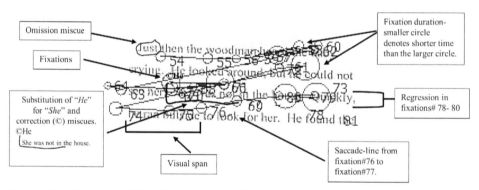

Figure 3.1: Example of Eye Movement and Miscue Measures

Source: Authors.
Source: Eye movement miscue measures are overlaid on a reading excerpt of *The man who kept house* (McInnes, 1962, p. 283).

Miscue Analysis Method

Miscue analysis is designed to identify and evaluate the strategies used by readers to process written material (Goodman, 1973; Y. Goodman et al., 2005). In miscue analysis, teachers/researchers examine readers' responses to the text in their oral reading, particularly when their responses differ from what is expected in the written text (i.e., their miscues). Miscue analysis studies consistently show that readers' miscues are never accidental or random but the result of how the readers predict and construct meaning by integrating cues from the language cueing systems: syntactic, semantic, and graphophonic (Goodman, 1973; Y. Goodman et al., 2005).

Teachers/researchers choose how to analyze readers' miscues from a variety of procedures. These include the classroom procedure and the in-depth procedure for miscue analysis (Y. Goodman et al., 2005). In the classroom procedure, each sentence within the entire text is analyzed as the linguistic unit, whether it includes miscues or not. For the in-depth procedure, each miscue is analyzed in relation to other miscues in the sentence and within the entire text. The analysis of sentences or miscues is based on the language cueing systems.

Miscue analysis always includes a retelling as a measure of comprehension. In the retelling, readers are first asked what they understood or remembered about what they have read (unaided retelling). Then, using the reader's own language from the retelling, the teacher/researcher asks open-ended questions to encourage the reader to expand on their unaided retellings. According to Y. Goodman et al.'s (2005) *Reading Miscue Inventory: From Evaluation to Instruction,* a retelling guide includes character analysis (character names and characterization) and story events (major and minor happenings or ideas broken into plot episodes).

Thus, by analyzing readers' miscues and retellings, teachers/researchers learn about readers' strengths and strategies and how effectively and efficiently they read the text with a focus on constructing meaning. Miscue Analysis measures are defined in Table 3.1.

Combining Eye Movement and Miscue Analysis: EMMA Method

Tracking the eyes over a visual stimulus illuminates what areas readers looked at and even fixated on, but it does not indicate how readers perceived/processed the information (K. Goodman et al., 2016). However, through EMMA, researchers can look at the fixations produced by a reader during reading and at the same time overlay that with their verbal production (see Figure 3.1), allowing them to gain "interpretive adequacy with both the nature of the eye movements and the stimulus source influencing verbal productions" (Nelson et al., 2008, p. 295). Thus, eye movement recordings in combination with dedicated oral reading analysis tools, allow for deeper insights into a reader's cognitive processing of texts.

EMMA researchers investigate reading in various ways, but for most, the structure for how data is collected and analyzed is framed in a transactional

Measure	Definition	Example
Miscue	An observed response that is different than the expected response	*the* ⓒ She untwists that ⟨little brown⟩ bag.
Retelling	To recap what happened in the text, using specific details and information stated in the text, after it is read	Peter wrote a letter to Amy. Amy saw it was for her so she was running to it, but Peter didn't want her to see it because he thought the surprise would be spoiled. Then Amy went running home crying and Peter thought she wasn't gonna come and she was sad for half of the party and he didn't think she was gonna come. But she came and she was happy for the rest of the party.

Type of Miscues	Definition	Example
Substitution	Oral replacement of a word/phrase/sentence for another	*started* Peter stared at the sheet of paper for a while.
Insertion	Oral addition of a word/phrase/sentence not found in the written text	*of cherry* It is the kind ∧ that is light red and sour.
Omission	Absence of a word/phrase/sentence in the reader's oral text	Put ⟨on⟩ a stamp.
Correction	Reader's spontaneous self-correction of a miscue	ⓒ *was* He saw his reflection in the street.
Repetition	Oral repetition of a section of text	Ⓡ She'd have to go get it.
Nonword	Miscue that is not recognizable as a word	*$frist* They explored the forest together.

Table 3.1: Miscue Analysis Measures

Note: Miscues are in italics; Substitution is written above the text; ^ denotes an Insertion; Omission is circled; c denotes a correction; R denotes a repetition; $ denotes a non-word (Based on Goodman, Watson, & Burke, 2005).

socio-psycholinguistic model of reading (K. Goodman et al., 2016; Y. Goodman et al., 2005). EMMA researchers usually examine eye movement measures in combination with oral readings that reveal common or unique patterns about how readers interact with texts (e.g., Duckett, 2001; Liwanag, 2010; Paulson, 2002; Paulson, Alexander, & Armstrong, 2007). They also use eye movement data such as fixations and saccades to triangulate observations from miscue analysis, retellings, and other reading protocols (e.g., think aloud, etc.) to explain participants' cognitive strategies (e.g., predicting, confirming, disconfirming) (Arya & Feathers, 2012; Brown, Kim, & O'Brien, 2012; Duckett, 2008; Feathers & Arya, 2012; Kim, Duckett, & Brown, 2010). Some researchers also explain eye movement and miscue patterns across specific identified areas of interest, such as a range of words from texts or pictorial images, to take note of patterns or unique observances of reader strategies to help understand the reading process (Feathers & Arya, 2015; Hung, 2019; Liwanag, Pelatti, P. Martens, & R. Martens, 2016). Thus, this hybrid form of analysis that combines patterns observed from the eye movement and miscue data has been used dynamically to provide insights about the process of reading.

EMMA as a Research Methodology Across Studies

Since EMMA as a research methodology was first utilized in literacy research studies, researchers have published numerous works showcasing the breadth and use of this combined methodology. In the following sections, we examine EMMA research across a 20-year span, using the EMMA forum bibliography database (www.emmaforum.org). Based on the articles, book chapters, and conference proceedings documented there, the research studies demonstrate diversity in terms of participants, their age ranges, types of texts, and languages. Additionally, the EMMA studies offer valuable insights about literacy curriculum and instruction and instruction in related fields.

Early EMMA Studies

Research studies conducted between 2000–2007 using EMMA focused on integrating Eye Movement and Miscue Analysis in the design and analysis processes (Duckett, 2001; Freeman, 2001; Paulson, 2000). This period marked the beginning of the use of EMMA to analyze how we read. The research studies established the data collection procedure where participants sat in front of the eye-tracking stimulus computer while reading a text. Oral readings were also simultaneously recorded for later examination. Usually two individuals were involved in data collection due to the complex set up of multiple monitors, video camera, and an audio recorder. Also, an adult was responsible for turning the pages for readers because when readers controlled the mouse, they usually looked down, resulting in lost data. Once data was collected, miscue analysis and eye fixation maps were juxtaposed, providing the researchers an estimate of when and how eye movements took place relative to miscues (Paulson, 2000). This allowed them to closely study patterns observed between the participants' eye movements, oral reading analysis, and retellings.

Researchers worked with earlier eye-tracking machines (e.g., ASL 504) that at that time were not as versatile and flexible when considering that the method involved having readers read a complete text. Limited capabilities of the eye-tracking machine with regards to readers' natural stances when reading, were among the earliest challenges EMMA researchers encountered. Despite these limitations, the early eye-tracking studies provided researchers with a novel view of how reading works.

Diversity in Participants, Texts, and Language

From 2008–2010, some research studies showed how using EMMA enabled researchers to reveal "misconceptions manifest in the clinical practice of intervention providers" for children with language impairment (Nelson et. al, 2008). Others examined the reading process of young and adult bilinguals in their readings of Spanish and Tagalog texts to show how all readers use reading strategies irrespective of language (Liwanag, 2010; Nelson et. al 2008). EMMA methodology was also used to provide information for preservice and K–12 teachers on comprehension (Paulson, 2008). Researchers published case studies about readers' strategies or their reading behaviors to demonstrate how reader strategies and comprehension were unmistakably linked in the combined miscue, eye, and retelling data.

Dedicated eye-tracking solutions (e.g., ASL D6, ASL D7, ASL Mobile Eye, SR EyeLink, Tobii Pro) during this period allowed measurement of eye movements in mobile, office, or lab environments, both outdoor and indoor, and day and night. This facilitated working with children of various ages and racial, cultural, and linguistic diversity. It also supported using different types of texts for data collection. Additionally, during this time, changes were made to the analysis software. Up until 2011, eye-tracking data could be viewed in static displays. The eye-tracking lab at Wayne State University in Michigan developed a data analysis software that allowed eye-tracking video data to be merged with audio from oral readings in real time. Other eye-tracking companies like ASL and the lab at the University of Arizona followed suit and developed similar data analysis software. This positively impacted researchers' ability to examine the reading process more closely.

Between 2011–2019, researchers used EMMA to examine readers' processing of various types of texts such as musical, science, multimodal, and picturebooks. For example, Liwanag and Jones (2011) used a musical text to explore music-sight reading; Hung (2014) and Hung, Kuo, Liao (2019) examined strategies young readers used as they read science texts; and Arya and Feathers (2012) had young children read two different versions of a picturebook to examine how readers used both the verbal and the visual information across texts. Liwanag and Dresbach (2012), Feathers and Arya (2015), and Liwanag, Pelatti, P. Martens, and R. Martens (2016) expanded this work by examining how we read multimodally. They used EMMA data and information from various sign systems to highlight the role that illustrations play in readers' construction of meaning during picturebook reading and help preservice teachers understand the dynamics of reading.

Eye movement data merged with oral reading and retelling data was also used to study older readers' reading strategies. Mantei and Kervin (2016) used EMMA to highlight the strategies a fifth grader applied during reading and how they impacted his meaning-making process. Similarly, Porter and colleagues (2019) used EMMA data to provide reading profiles of two college readers as they read informational texts.

Other researchers have used EMMA to collaborate with parents and demonstrate for them how reading works and influences "family's beliefs and lived experiences as readers" (Kim & Meyer, 2017, p. 172). Finally, some studies have used EMMA to understand children's reading in other languages, such as Chinese (Hung, 2019) and Japanese (Ferguson, Kato, & Nagahiro, 2012; Kim, 2012), highlighting the robustness of EMMA as a methodology to study the reading process.

Future Avenues for EMMA Research

Future research using EMMA can extend beyond oral readings and retellings to include other modes like silent reading and online reading. Additionally, researchers can use other research protocols such as think-alouds or writing response strategies. Another area for expanding EMMA research includes studying metacognition through retrospective eye movement miscue analysis (REMMA). Additionally, EMMA as a research methodology can be used in interdisciplinary and transdisciplinary studies across various fields beyond education. Enhanced collaborations with computer science, math, political science, and health sciences, to name a few, can enrich other avenues for how reading as a meaning-making process is universal and indispensable in the current global world.

References

Applied Science Laboratories (2015). *Eye tracker systems manual* (Version 3.3). Billerica, MA.

Arya, P., & Feathers, K. (2012). Reconsidering children's readings: Insights into the reading process. *Reading Psychology, 33*(4), 301–322.

Brown, J., Kim, K., & O'Brien Ramirez, K. (2012). What a teacher hears, what a reader sees: Eye movements from a phonics-taught second grader. *Journal of Early Childhood Literacy, 12*(2), 202–222.

Buswell, G. (1936). *How people look at pictures: A study of the psychology of perception in art.* Chicago: The University of Chicago Press.

Duchowski, A. (2002). A breadth-first survey of eye-tracking applications. *Behavior Research Methods, Instruments, & Computers, 34*(4), 455–470.

Duckett, P. (2001*). First-grade beginning readers' use of pictures and print as they read: A miscue analysis and eye movement study* (Unpublished doctoral dissertation). University of Arizona, Tucson, Arizona.

Duckett, P. (2002). New insights: Eye fixations and the reading process. *Talking Points, 13*(2), 16–21.

Duckett, P. (2008). Seeing the story for the words: The eye movements of beginning readers. In A. D. Flurkey, E. J. Paulson, & K. S. Goodman, (Eds.), *Scientific realism in studies of reading* (pp. 113–128). Mahwah, NJ: Lawrence Erlbaum Associates.

Ehrlich, S. F., & Rayner, K. (1981). Contextual effects on word perception and eye movements during reading. *Journal of Memory and Language, 20*(6), 641–655.

Feathers, K., & Arya, P. (2012). The role of illustrations during children's reading. *Journal of Children's Literature, 38*(1), 36–43.

Feathers, K., & Arya, P. (2015). Exploring young children's use of illustrations in a picturebook. *Language and Literacy, 17*(1), 42–62.

Ferguson, D., Kato, Y., & Nagahiro, M. (2012). Miscues and eye movements of Japanese beginner readers. In K. Goodman, S. Wang, M. Iventosch, & Y. Goodman (Eds.), *Reading in Asian languages: Making sense of written texts in Chinese, Japanese, and Korean* (pp. 127–143). New York, NY: Routledge.

Freeman, A. (2001). *The eyes have it: Oral miscue and eye movement analyses of the reading of fourth-grade Spanish/English bilinguals* (Unpublished doctoral dissertation). University of Arizona, Tucson, Arizona.

Goodman, K. S. (1973). Miscues: Windows on the reading process. In K. S. Goodman (Ed.), *Miscue analysis: Applications to reading instruction.* Urbana, IL: ERIC Clearinghouse on Reading and Communication Skills, National Council of Teachers of English.

Goodman, K., Fries, P. H., & Strauss, S. L. (2016). *Reading, the grand illusion: How and why people make sense of print.* New York: Routledge.

Goodman, Y. M., Watson, D. J., & Burke, C. L. (2005). *Reading miscue inventory: From evaluation to instruction.* Katonah, NY: Richard C. Owen Publishers.

Holmqvist, K., Nystrom, M., Anderson, R., Dewhurst, R., Jarodzka, H., van de Weijer, J. (2015). *Eye tracking: A comprehensive guide to methods and measures.* Oxford: Oxford University Press.

Huey, E. (1900). On the psychology and physiology of reading. *American Journal of Psychology, 11*, 283–302.

Hung, Y. (2014). "What are you looking at?" An eye movement exploration in science text reading. *International Journal of Science and Mathematics Education, 12*(2), 241–260.

Hung, Y. (2019). Fifth grade students reading a Chinese text with embedded errors: An eye movement miscue analysis study. *Reading Psychology, 40*(5), 397–424.

Hung, Y., Kuo, H., & Liao, S. (2019). Seeing what they see: Elementary EFL students reading science texts. *RELC Journal.* Retrieved from https://doi.org/10.1177/0033688219854475.

Inhoff, A. W., Pollatsek, A., Posner, M. I., & Rayner, K. (1989). Covert attention and eye movements during reading. *Quarterly Journal of Experimental Psychology, 41*(1-A), 63–89.

iView ETG portable by SMI (2016). iView ETG Portable [Brochure]. Retrieved from http://www.humre.vu.lt/files/doc/Instrukcijos/SMI/ETG.pdf.

Just, M. A., & Carpenter, P. A. (1980). A theory of reading: From eye fixations to comprehension. *Psychological Review, 87*(4), 329–354.

Kim, K. (2012). How readers process Japanese orthography in two different texts. In K. Goodman, S. Wang, M. Iventosch, & Y. Goodman (Eds.), *Reading in Asian languages: Making sense of written texts in Chinese, Japanese, and Korean* (pp. 144–157). New York: Routledge.

Kim, K., Duckett, P., & Brown, J. (2010). Reframing the reading process through EMMA (Eye movement miscue analysis). *Talking Points, 22*(1), 10–14.

Kim, K., & Meyer, R. (2017). Two curricular worlds: Home and school. In *Reclaiming early childhood literacies: Narratives of hope, power, and vision* (pp. 169–179). New York: Routledge.

Liwanag, M. (2010). Reading patterns in the eye movement miscue analysis of adult bilingual readers. In L. Gomez Chavo & D. Belenguer (Eds.), *International Conference of Education, Research and Innovation Proceedings* (pp. 2178–2183). Valencia, Spain: IATED.

Liwanag, M., & Dresbach, S. (2012). Reading multimodally: Designing and developing multimedia literacy projects through an understanding of eye movement miscue analysis. *Journal of Interactive Technology and Pedagogy.* Retrieved from https://jitp.commons.gc.cuny.edu/reading-multimodally-designing-and-developing-multimedia-literacy-projects-through-an-understanding-of-eye-movement-miscue-analysis-emma/.

Liwanag, M., & Jones, W. (2011). Transforming teaching and learning by engaging in music eye movement and miscue analysis research. In *International Conference of Education, Research and Innovation Proceedings* (pp. 2746–2750). Madrid, Spain: IATED.

Liwanag, M., Martens, P., Martens, R., & Pelatti, C. (2017). Examining a reader's meaning-making process with picturebooks using eye movement miscue analysis. *Literacy Research: Theory, Method, and Practice, 66*(1), 248–263.

Liwanag, M., Pelatti, C., Martens, P., & Martens, R., (2016). Children's eye movements, miscue analysis patterns, and retellings when reading a counterpoint picturebook. *Literacy Research: Theory, Method, and Practice, 65*(1), 253–267.

Liversedge, S., Gilchrist, I., & Everling, S. (2011). *The Oxford handbook of eye movements*. Oxford: Oxford University Press.

Mantei, J., & Kervin, L. K. (2016). Tracking eye movements to gain insights into an older reader's reading practices. *The Middle Years, 24*(3), 36–44.

McConkie, G. W., & Rayner, K. (1975). The span of the effective stimulus during a fixation in reading. *Perception & Psychophysics, 17*(6), 578–586.

Nelson, R. L., Damico, J. S., & Smith, S. K. (2008). Applying eye movement miscue analysis to the reading patterns of children with language impairment. *Clinical Linguistics & Phonetics, 22*(4–5), 293–303.

Özyurt, J., DeSouza, P., West, P., Rutschmann, R., & Greenlee, M. W. (2001, August). *Comparison of cortical activity and oculomotor performance in the gap and step paradigms.* Paper presented at the European Conference on Visual Perception (ECVP), Kusadasi, Turkey.

Paulson, E. (2000). *Adult readers' eye movements during the production of oral miscues* (Unpublished dissertation). University of Arizona, Tucson, Arizona.

Paulson, E. (2002). Are oral reading word omissions and substitutions caused by careless eye movements? *Journal of Reading Psychology, 23*(1), 45–66.

Paulson, E. (2005). Viewing eye movements during reading through the lens of chaos theory: How reading is like the weather. *Reading Research Quarterly, 40*(3), 338–358.

Paulson, E. & Freeman, A. (2003). *Insight from the eyes: The science of effective reading instruction.* Portsmouth, NH: Heinemann.

Paulson, E., Alexander, J., & Armstrong, S. (2007). Peer review re-viewed: Investigating the juxtaposition of composition students' eye movements and peer-review processes. *Research in the Teaching of English, 41*(3), 304–335.

Paulson, E. (2008). Miscues and eye movements: Functions of comprehension. In A. D. Flurkey, E. J. Paulson, & K. S. Goodman, (Eds.), *Scientific realism in studies of reading* (pp. 247–264). Mahwah, NJ: Lawrence Erlbaum Associates.

Porter, H., Kim, K., Franzak, J., & MacDonald, K. (2020). Reframing and repositioning college readers' assumptions about reading through eye movement miscue analysis. *Journal of Adolescent & Adult Literacy, 63*(5), 519–528.

Rayner, K. (1975). The perceptual span and peripheral cues in reading. *Cognitive Psychology, 7*, 65–81.

Rayner, K. (1998). Eye movements in reading and information processing: 20 years of research. *Psychological Bulletin, 124*(3), 372–422.

Rayner, K. (2009). Eye movements and attention in reading, scene perception, and visual search. *Quarterly Journal of Experimental Psychology, 62*(8), 1457–1506.

Rayner, K., & Bertera, J. H. (1979). Reading without a fovea. *Science, 206*(4417), 468–469.

Rayner, K., Slattery, T. J., & Bélanger, N. N. (2010). Eye movements, the perceptual span, and reading speed. *Psychonomic Bulletin & Review, 17*(6), 834–839.

Reichle, E. D., Pollatsek, A., Fisher, D. L., & Rayner, K. (1998). Toward a model of eye movement control in reading. *Psychological Review, 105*(1), 125–157.

SensoMotoric Instruments (2016). *iViewETG User Guide.* Retrieved from http://www.humre.vu.lt/files/doc/Instrukcijos/SMI/ETG.pdf.

SR Research (2017). *EyeLink 1000 Plus: Multiple Eye tracking in One Manual.* Ontario, ON, Canada: SR Research. Retrieved from https://www.sr-research.com/wp-content/uploads/2018/01/EyeLink-1000-Plus-Brochure.pdf

SR Research (2017a). *EyeLink Portable Duo Manual.* Ontario, ON, Canada: SR Research. Retrieved from https://www.sr-research.com/wp-content/uploads/2017/07/EyeLink-Portable-Duo-Brochure-2016-10-27.pdf.

Tobii Pro X3-120 (n.d.). *Tobii Pro [Brochure].* Retrieved from https://www.tobiipro.com/siteassets/tobii-pro/brochures/tobiipro-x3-120-brochure.pdf/?v=1.0.

Appendix A: List of Eye-Tracking Machines Used in EMMA Research

The eye-tracking machines used by EMMA researchers are described below. The descriptions have been taken from the user manuals for the various eye trackers:

Applied Science Laboratories Model 504, D6, D7-Eye Trackers (2015). These eye trackers are designed to measure a person's pupil diameter and point of gaze on a stationary stimulus. The auto-focus eye camera and the eye illuminator (IR beam) are contained in a pan-tilt module. The pan-tilt mechanism provides about 100° of pan angle and 25° of tilt capability. ASL eye trackers pan/tilt optics records data at the rate of 50 or 60 Hz. The eye-tracking device is placed below the computer monitor the subject is viewing. These systems also include a Magnetic Head Tracker that tracks the position of the subject's head, including head rotation. Additionally, a Gaze Tracker or Paradigm software can be programmed to control the stimulus display, timing, and data recording output.

The EyeLink Portable Duo by SR Research (2017). This eye tracker is a portable eye-tracking system with dual use data collection modes. It can be used in the head-stabilized mode or remote head free-to-move mode. The EyeLink tracker consists of a high-speed camera connected to a dedicated Host computer that records data at the rate of 2000Hz with the head stabilized or 1000Hz with the head free-to-move mode. EyeLink Data Viewer is a powerful software package that is used for viewing, filtering, and processing gaze data recorded with EyeLink eye trackers. (https://www.sr-research.com/wp-content/uploads/2017/07/EyeLink-Portable-Duo-Brochure-2016-10-27.pdf)

The EyeLink 1000 by SR Research (2017a). This is a customizable eye tracker with multiple mounting options, interchangeable lenses, and multiple head free-to-move remote configurations. An infrared illuminator is also available for low visibility environments. It has a sampling rate of up to or 2000Hz with the head stabilized or 1000Hz in the remote option. EyeLink Data Viewer is a powerful software package that is used for viewing, filtering, and processing gaze data recorded with EyeLink eye trackers. (https://www.sr-research.com/wp-content/uploads/2018/01/EyeLink-1000-Plus-Brochure.pdf)

iView ETG portable by SMI (2016). iView ETG portable is a mobile eye-tracking equipment with a 60hz/120Hz sampling rate. This binocular tracking device has two small cameras on the rim of the glasses (one camera recording the left eye and one camera recording the right eye) and a scene camera on the front of the glasses. The equipment records eye movements with audio and video data. BeGaze is used as the software to analyze eye movement data from this device. (http://www.humre.vu.lt/files/doc/Instrukcijos/SMI/ETG.pdf)

Tobii Pro X3-120 (n.d.). This is a standalone eye tracker that can be used with a variety of set-ups by attaching it to monitors and laptops. It is an unobtrusive eye tracker that allows the subject to move during recording while maintaining accuracy and precision. It has a sampling rate of 120hz. It measures about 324mm (12.7") in length and weighs 118 grams (4.2 oz.). This eye tracker has infrared diodes to generate reflection patterns on the corneas of the subject's eyes that are collected by the image sensor. Algorithms and mathematical computations are used to identify relevant patterns for the eye position and the gaze point on the screen or where the participant is looking. (https://www.tobiipro.com/siteassets/tobii-pro/brochures/tobiipro-x3-120-brochure.pdf/?v=1.0)

Part III

Reading Process and Strategies

4

Using Eye Movement Miscue Analysis (EMMA) to Explore Children's Reading Strategies During Periods of Extended Pauses

by Jessica Mantei and Lisa Kervin

This chapter draws from extensive knowledge of print-based reading developed over many years by multiple scholars across multiple continents. There is general agreement that children learn to read through language activities comprising exposure to a range of texts, opportunities to interact with and examine texts, and time to practice reading skills and strategies. There is also consensus that meaning making is the purpose of reading.

Despite these extended understandings, the reality is that many children struggle to develop reading proficiency. Proficient readers are independent and judicious users of problem-solving skills and strategies applied in response to the range of demands presented in text (Anderson & Kaye, 2017; Clay, 1991; Goodman, Watson, & Burke, 2005). Proficient readers respond to information, monitor responses, and make meaning by detecting and correcting their responses when meaning is lost. Researchers (i.e., Andersen & Kaye, 2017; Goodman, 1996; Goodman, et al., 2005) argue less proficient readers use the same processes, but their integration and application of those sources are limited in flexibility and sophistication.

Purposes and Processes of Reading Assessments

School-based reading assessments are informed by existing beliefs about proficiency and have focused primarily on assessing word solving skills. That is, readers are assessed on their ability to interpret symbolic representations of oral language in connection with the grammatical structures, topic, and text content. The selection of reading assessments has been led by practical aspects pertaining to text format (e.g., number of words), administration (e.g., time taken), and information offered (e.g., reading levels), providing teachers with little access to tools for analysis of cognitive processes for meaning making.

Children's reading is typically assessed in classrooms by teachers who make "inferences about the nature of a student's reading from a sample of their reading behaviour" (Afflerbach, 2016, p. 413). Assessments related to teacher evaluation of proficiency are usually aligned with criterion-referenced lists in a basal curriculum designed to track progress (Deno, Marston, Shinn & Tindal, 1983). While we acknowledge the importance of teacher evaluation, relying predominantly on verbal utterances on carefully scaffolded basal texts to assess reading is problematic (Mantei & Kervin, 2016).

Increasingly, reading assessment has focused on measuring a reader's comprehension. For example, *miscue analysis* (Goodman, 1996) uses a read and retell strategy to examine a reader's process and comprehension. After the reading, verbal responses are analyzed to gain insight into information sources used (Goodman et al., 2005). Of particular interest are miscues—responses differing from the printed text—because they inform future pedagogies. The subsequent retell offers opportunities to assess comprehension because it represents an "independent construction from transacting with a text" (Kucer, 2014, p. 32).

While analyses of miscues and retellings offer important insights into a reader's comprehension of a text, other indicators of understanding, such as orchestration (Clay, 1991), must also be acknowledged. Orchestrated reading is considered a demonstration of comprehension because it requires the reader to "bring together" all sources of information at a conversational rate and with appropriate expression (Clay, 1991; Hudson, Lane, & Pullen, 2005). As such, an interruption or pause implies disruption in comprehension. In this chapter we argue that analysing reading pauses offers new opportunities for understanding reading development.

New Opportunities for Understanding Reading Development

Technology affords the development of new assessment techniques, and eye movement technologies offer new perspectives on reading when a child becomes silent. Extended silences or pauses are significant because until now, when a child becomes silent during reading, educators have had little information to use as they plan their next teaching intervention.

This research project uses the long-established reading miscue inventory (RMI), a reading assessment (Goodman et al., 2005) underpinned by sociocultural theories of learning that view reading as a unique transaction between a physical reading resource and the experiences, beliefs, and knowledge a person brings to the reading event (Rosenblatt, 1982). Within this transaction, the reader responds to cues in an effort to make meaning. An unexpected/observed response—one that differs from the precise information on the page—allows the educator to consider the reader's use of "cues" or information sources in the meaning making process (Goodman et al., 2005).

While RMI is not new, combining it with eye movement technology affords new insights into reading development, potentially challenging established theoretical assumptions. Previous research emerging from eye movement with miscue analysis (EMMA) revealed that the reading path is not predetermined, word-by-word, or regular. Paulson (2002) and Liwanag, Martens, Martens, and Pelatti (2017a) argue that emergent and proficient readers sample only parts of the text on a page. Arya and Feathers (2012) and Liwanag and colleagues (2017b) found reading efficiency improved, with fewer fixations and shorter fixation durations when the content was familiar for any reader. And, Arya and Feathers (2012) further found that teachers were limited in their ability to support development without deep understandings about the ways readers use "verbal and visual components" (p. 301).

Previous EMMA research used statistical data to examine gaze, saccades, and fixations to develop theoretical understandings about the complexity and non-linearity of reading. And it is these important insights that inform our perspective. Our project used eye movement data to examine readers' strategies when they encountered something unknown and they paused. We problematize reading theory by examining young readers' activity when it appears they are doing nothing at all.

As such, in this chapter we ask: (1) What can eye movement data reveal about a child's reading strategies during periods of extended pauses? and (2) What implications are there for reading pedagogies?

Conducting the Study

The School Site

We conducted our research in a regional primary school in New South Wales (NSW), Australia. The state education department required teachers at this school to deliver specialized programs and submit specific data to a central repository for government monitoring. Teachers mapped literacy development against the state-based literacy continuum, a scope and sequence of literacy skills for each elementary school grade, Kindergarten to Grade 6. The scope and sequence categorizes literacy skills into developmental groups aligned with student learning at each grade. Teachers then plot each child's progress into these developmental groupings along the continuum. Like many others in

NSW, this school had plotted all students' reading progress into developmental groups informed by assessments using levelled basal texts.

Our Research Approach

Previous EMMA research has been located in laboratories. Researchers reproduced pages of texts on a computer screen and tracked participants' eye movements with equipment located in the monitor, allowing an examination of the length of a fixation and numbers of saccades. Findings from this important lab-based work have demystified beliefs about reading English print as a systematic practice of processing text left to right.

Our research focuses on reading in classrooms where individuals and small groups engage in often noisy collaborative planned and spontaneous learning experiences, allowing us to challenge traditional reading theories and pedagogies. Our participants wore portable eye tracking glasses and the research team administered RMI assessments in classrooms during regular language arts lessons. Children were invited to "read as though they were reading alone" (Goodman et al., 2005, p. 53) so independent processes could be examined. The children were assessed as they read the types of texts generally available in school classrooms: part of a novel, a picturebook, factual texts, and an ebook.

Selection of Texts for EMMA Assessment. Since text selection is key to success in any lesson, we analyzed and selected texts using an adaptation of Fountas and Pinnell's (1996) text difficulty guide, matched against the state-based literacy continuum. Our analysis considered the ways each text could support a less proficient reader while presenting challenges that would prompt the activation of problem-solving strategies.

Our Readers. Teachers identified readers in grades two to six (7–12 years old) who were reading below grade average. Consequently, we gathered data from 30 children through 54 EMMA assessments over six weeks (see Table 4.1).

Twelve children completed a single assessment, twelve completed two, and six completed three. The number of texts read depended on availability, preference for ongoing participation, and analysis of previous assessments. For example, Grade 2 student Sanjay read an information text (*Teeth and Fangs*) during one assessment and then a narrative (*My Uncle's Donkey*) in another, affording insights into his responses across different structures and language features.

This chapter examines new insights afforded by eye movement technology in periods of extended pauses as further evidence about a child's reading development. Pillai and Paramasivam (2014) define a "hesitation" as a pause of three to five seconds, and an extended pause is defined as any non-verbal response longer than five seconds. Since the intention during RMI assessments is to

Students and Developmental group	Texts used for assessment	Extended pauses
Grade 2		
5 students	My Uncle's Donkey	15
Group 4-5	Teeth and Fangs	
Grade 3		
9 students	My Uncle's Donkey	16
Group 5-8	Looking for Crabs	
	Stanley, Flat again	
	Teeth and Fangs	
Grade 4		
5 students	Looking for Crabs	3
Group 8-9	Stanley, Flat Again	
	Mammals	
Grade 5		
3 students	My Uncle's Donkey	14
Group 8-9	Teeth and Fangs	
	Mammals	
	Looking for Crabs	
	Herman Rosie eBook	
Grade 6		
8 students	Looking for Crabs	4
Group 8-10	Stanley, Flat Again	
	My Uncle's Donkey	
	Snakes	
	Mammals	
Totals		
30 participants	54 assessments	52 extended pauses

Table 4.1: Participant Summary

Source: Authors

leave the reading uninterrupted (Goodman et al., 2005), periods of silence are common as readers are left to their own resources to address reading puzzles. There was a considerable volume of extended periods of silence (n=52) well beyond five seconds in our data (average pause=31 seconds), and as such, we propose that a focus on extended pauses offers opportunities to generate new knowledge about the ways we understand the reading process.

Understanding Our Data

We analyzed instances of extended pauses (n=52) using RMI, eye movement and retell data.

Miscue Analysis. We analyzed readers' miscues using the in-depth procedure, coding substitutions, omissions, insertions, repetitions, re-reading, and corrections for the use of semantic, syntactic and graphophonic information sources (Goodman et al., 2005).

Retelling. We transcribed the unaided and aided retellings verbatim to examine the reader's comprehension. A Retelling Summary Form (Goodman et al., 2005) allowed us to analyze the comprehension of plots and themes, inferences, and misconceptions evident in each retell (Goodman et al., 2005, p. 250), particularly at the point of an extended pause. We then mapped these against RMI codes and eye movement data, giving us multiple perspectives on each child's reading process.

Eye Movement. To improve tracking accuracy, we used a 3-point calibration for the iView ETG portable equipment. This equipment records eye movements, audio, and video data, giving a recording of the oral reading and a video of the child's view within the busy classroom. Using BeGaze 3.4 (2014) semantic gaze mapping, we identified extended pauses and eye movements from that period mapped against the video display of the corresponding pages in the text. We then analyzed tracked eye movements for each reader's problem-solving strategies. Bringing the analyses together, we generated categories related to our research questions.

What We Learned

Extended pauses fell into two categories plus outliers across 52 instances:

- *Category 1:* extended pauses followed by an omission, either of a word, the remaining section of a line, or the page itself

- *Category 2:* extended pauses followed by a low-quality substitution, that is, responses that were semantically unacceptable, made little sense, or, in some cases, nonsense words

- *Outliers:* one extended pause resulted in a high-quality substitution and one a correct response. While noted, these are not the focus of this chapter.

It was during extended pauses where the readers appeared inactive that we observed eye movements and drew insights into the reading strategies readers were attempting to apply. We now share one case from each category to explore the nature of extended pauses and the reading strategies evident. For Category 1, we chose Sanjay as he accrued the most instances (n=7) among all participants, while eight of Kayden's ten extended pauses fit with Category 2, again, the most of all participants.

Category 1: Extended Pauses Followed by Omissions

RMI data revealed that 32 instances of extended pauses averaging 25 seconds across 54 assessments led to omissions of a word, line or the rest of the page. A sample of Grade 2 student, Sanjay's reading explicates the nature of eye movements in Category 1.

Sanjay's teacher placed him in developmental group five (Grade 1). When reading *My Uncle's Donkey* (Riddle, 2010) he omitted 28 of 174 words, mainly prepositional phrases locating the sites of the donkey's activities, e.g., *in the kitchen.* While he corrected three of 13 substitutions, uncorrected substitutions revealed Sanjay responded to initial and sometimes final letters in a word along with some semantic and syntactic information. For example, the text read, *My uncle's donkey has a favourite chair.* Sanjay substituted *fancy* for *favourite,* and *couch* for *chair* and read, *My uncle's donkey has a fancy couch,* which we coded as high quality miscues.

Sanjay recalled the donkey's activities he had read aloud (e.g., watching movies), including the activities that he had omitted in the reading. This is not surprising given the eye movement data revealed Sanjay in extended study of all illustrations on all pages.

Of Sanjay's five extended pauses (average=36 seconds), all led to omissions of the remaining text on that page. Sanjay's first extended pause provides insights into his solving strategies. On line 09, *My uncle's donkey does hoofstands in the kitchen,* the illustration shows the uncle, center foreground at the kitchen table, back to the donkey. Behind him, the donkey performs a "hoofstand." Sanjay read, *My uncle's donkey,* repeated *donkey,* paused for 59 seconds, reread *My uncle's donkey* and paused for a further 31 seconds. When he continued to make no response, we prompted him to do as he would if he were reading alone. Sanjay turned the page, omitting the remainder of the sentence, including the facing page.

A closer look at what happens in these 90 seconds provides greater insight into Sanjay's strategies. Limitations in the affordances of the analysis software have prevented markings to be made on Figures 4.1–4.4. However, we have captured the reading in smaller chunks of time and provided extended descriptions of the processes observed. Figure 4.1 captures Sanjay's eye movements during the first 19 seconds of reading time, while Figure 4.2 captures his eye movements from the 42nd to 59th second of the same reading period, all of which occurred as an extended pause.

While Sanjay made no verbal responses during the extended pauses, eye movement data revealed him hard at work. The initial 10 seconds of reading (see Figure 4.1) capture a typical reading pattern where Sanjay initially looked at and read aloud the beginning of the sentence, *My uncle's donkey*. After this initial 10 seconds, he paused. His eye movements (shown in Figure 4.1) revealed that after 10 seconds, he omitted *does* and turned his attention to *hoofstands*, followed by a scan of the illustration, all without saying anything. After 19 seconds, still having only read aloud the initial three words of the sentence, it became evident in Sanjay's eyes movements (see Figure 4.1) that he was using a range of reading strategies. For example, he reread the sentence from the beginning, read on to the end of the sentence, and glanced to the donkey's hoof in the image, all without reading aloud. His use of the image and specifically looking to the donkey's hoof implies a developing understanding of the difficulty and that *hoofstand* is unfamiliar. After 19 seconds on this part of the text, it seems Sanjay's challenge related to vocabulary rather than his lack of reading strategies.

Sanjay continued to work on this text without reading aloud. From the 20th to 41st second, his eye movements reveal an interrogation of all print from beginning to end of the clause *My uncle's donkey does hoofstands in the kitchen*, demonstrating an understanding that the message is there. And after almost a

My uncle's donkey does hoofstands in the kitchen

and cartwheels in the living room.

Figure 4.1: Sanjay's Eye Movements During 19 Seconds of an Extended Pause (Riddle, 2010, pp. 7–8)

Source: Authors.

Source: By arrangement with the Licensor, Tohby Riddle, c/- Curtis Brown (Aust) Pty Ltd]

full minute (Figure 4.2 captures the 42nd–59th second of this extended pause), Sanjay had reread the text, searched all parts of the print, read on to the end of the sentence, and widened his search to the illustration on the facing page.

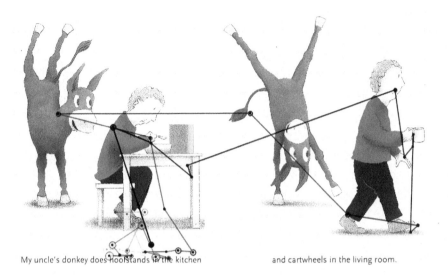

My uncle's donkey does hoofstands in the kitchen   and cartwheels in the living room.

Figure 4.2: Sanjay's Eye Movements Showing 42nd– 59th Seconds of an Extended Pause (Riddle, 2010, pp. 7–8)

Source: Authors.
Source: By arrangement with the Licensor, Tohby Riddle, c/- Curtis Brown (Aust) Pty Ltd]

Eye movement data reveals Sanjay was indeed a busy reader who looked to all sources of information. He worked outward from the problem, rereading, reading on, scanning illustrations and then extending his analysis for further information. Sanjay's thorough examination demonstrates his understanding that solutions come from a range of sources. However, he appears unable to bring the sources together, which impacted his ability to recall elements of this story. Sanjay did not identify that the donkey performed hoofstands in the kitchen.

Category 2: Extended Pauses Followed by Low Quality Substitutions
RMI data for the Category 2 example reveals 18 instances of extended pauses (average=42 seconds) followed by low-quality substitutions (Goodman et al., 2005), that is, substitutions that disrupt meaning.

Kayden's (Grade 5) teacher plotted his reading in developmental group nine, commensurate with Grade 3. On reading *Snake* (Watts, 2002), Kayden corrected three of 13 miscues, and responded to initial and final letters on the remaining 10. While his predictions were syntactically sound, e.g., maintaining plurals, they demonstrated his willingness to accept semantic discrepancies and even nonsense words. Kayden recalled two facts unprompted and three with prompts such as, *What can you tell me about the number of eggs a snake lays?*

Kayden's four extended pauses (average=60 seconds) led to low-quality substitutions drawn predominantly from graphophonic and syntactic information. The first provides an example through which to examine his reading strategies. Lines 02–04 and an accompanying photograph read, *Snake eggs are about 25 millimetres long and have a soft leathery shell.* Kayden read, *Snake eggs are about 25 milli-metres long and have a s-s-soft,* paused for 2:19 minutes before substituting *heavy* for *leathery* and reading quickly and correctly to the end of the page. Analysis of the substitution of *heavy* for *leathery* shows partial medial and final graphophonic similarity and syntactic consistency, but to suggest a 25 millimetre egg is heavy was judged semantically inconsistent.

Kayden made no sound during this extended pause, and we did not interrupt. Figures 4.3 and 4.4 capture eye movements at nine seconds and at 46 seconds into the pause at *leathery*. By nine seconds (Figure 4.3), Kayden had examined all parts of *leathery*, read on and reread the line. The mass of tracking points in Figure 4.3 captures the activity of those nine seconds, demonstrating the range of strategies Kayden has already used to solve this problem.

Figure 4.3: Kayden's Eye Movements on His Substitution of "Heavy" for "Leathery" After Nine Seconds of an Extended Pause (Watts, 2002, pp. 4–5)

Source: Authors.
Source: Watts, B. (2002). *Snake.* UK: Franklin Watts.

At 46 seconds (Figure 4.4), Kayden had repeated the strategies he used previously over and over without success and had not read anything aloud. Apart from glancing at both images, Kayden spent most of the time examining all parts of *leathery*, reading on, rereading, and eventually substituting *heavy* before reading on. *Heavy* had some graphophonic similarity to *leathery* and was syntactically acceptable but not semantically acceptable. The dense eye tracking lines covering "leathery shell" show his eye movements in this section, and hence his commitment to trying to solve this unknown part of the text. In his retell, Kayden could not explain that the eggs were heavy.

Figure 4.4: Kayden's Eye Movements on His Substitution of "Heavy" for "Leathery" After 46 Seconds of an Extended Pause (Watts, 2002, pp. 4–5)

Source: Authors.
Source: Watts, B. (2002). *Snake*. UK: Franklin Watts.

Kayden shows that he is an active reader prepared to spend significant time grappling with reading puzzles. He demonstrates resilience, an understanding that meaning is captured in print, and the capacity to retain meaning over an extended time. Kayden appears to have exhausted his repertoire of reading skills and strategies. The eye movement data during an extended pause demonstrates his attempt to draw information from a range of sources including the graphophonics of the troublesome text, the structures of the sentence, the images and the topic of the text. Further, it shows he applied the strategies proficient readers apply: he reread and read on, looked at all parts of the problem text, checked the picture and other relevant information such as the title, and eventually used a substitution that allowed him to continue. Perhaps the real reading challenge for Kayden here is a limited vocabulary that could support him to read this informative and more technical text.

Discussion

Responding to our first research question, the EMMA data gives insights into reading strategies during extended pauses. While external appearances suggest a reader in an extended pause is doing nothing or passively awaiting assistance, eye movement data revealed reading on, rereading, checking the image, searching all parts of a problem text, predicting, monitoring, and checking. As such, these findings align with Goodman's (1996) observation that proficient and less proficient readers apply the same reading strategies.

Extended pauses appear to indicate a struggle borne not from lack of knowledge about reading strategies, but by knowing how to use them. From 52 extended pauses, one led to a high-quality miscue and one to a correction, while the remaining 50 resulted in omissions or low-quality substitutions. This points to inefficiency in applying the meaning making strategies (Goodman, 1996). It seems these less proficient readers had limited understanding about reading strategies for increasingly complex and cross-disciplinary texts.

One example of this limitation is the considerable time spent examining images for clues. Using images relates to accessing semantic resources and is a valid solving strategy. It is generally learned early in the reading process with basal readers where images literally reflect print—if the print states "Baby Bear is in the river," the image conveys the same information. Early reading pedagogy includes the prompt to check the picture as a semantic clue (Clay, 1991), and on simple contrived texts, this usually provides access to the noun. While this is clearly supportive, a danger is that the reader will develop an over reliance on this strategy, a false understanding about the type of work readers do, and a narrow view about the role of images in text. Since more complex and nuanced literature utilizes augmentation or contradiction to generate sophisticated literary messages such as irony or humor, a greater understanding is required about "how to look" (Clay, 1991) with increasing sophistication and discrimination across disciplines, genre, and media.

Implications for Reading Pedagogies

If we accept the premise that a text is static and that meaning is made through the transactions between the reader's knowledge and the text, then we can acknowledge that different texts present different challenges (Liwanag et al., 2017a). Rosenblatt's (1982) observation that readers draw on existing repertoires of knowledge, experience, and skills offers a challenge for teachers to utilize reading pedagogies that build proficient repertoires. Traditionally, teachers are encouraged to prompt readers to use information source/s apparently neglected in an effort to progress the reading with minimal disruption. But the eye movement data showed our readers already attempting to use all sources of information, meaning teachers need to know more about the reader's process (Arya & Feathers, 2012; Mantei & Kervin, 2016).

Pedagogies that focus less on providing the clue for solving a puzzle in favor of those that invite a metacognitive response could reveal the reader's existing knowledge, and hence the next teaching step. For example, a prompt to Kayden, such as "I can see you're working hard. What are you thinking about in this section?" may reveal key information related to his vocabulary, morphological knowledge, or knowledge about information text structures. A greater understanding of the ways strategies are applied offers clear opportunities to teach new information about how texts work (Afflerbach, 2016; Anderson & Kaye, 2017).

We encourage teachers as proficient readers to reveal to their students the ways they apply strategies beyond the early ones related to processing of letters, sounds, and literal images. Since reading is mostly an internal process, it seems pedagogies that take an overt focus on explicating those processes offer a way forward. The well-established "think-aloud" protocol offers one solution because it provides explicit demonstrations of the questions proficient readers mentally pose as they read, reread, and gather information for solving reading puzzles. For example, from his reading of *My Uncle's Donkey*, Sanjay would benefit from a focus on the ways creative language and devices feature in imaginative texts, which could include made-up words such as "hoofstands." The think-aloud protocol could begin conversations not only about how proficient readers respond to difficult text, but also about their approach to increasingly sophisticated grammatical structures and vocabulary; to imaginative, persuasive, and technical language; and to the ways images work in connection with the print and for different purposes across texts.

Concluding Comments

One role of teachers is to support the development of reading practices that enable learners to participate as active members of their schools, their local communities, and the broader world. The findings shared in this chapter have expanded our understandings of this role in connection with the development of effective reading strategies. The findings point to the need for educators to engage pedagogies that make transparent the mental processes of proficient readers and to support the development of those processes in their learners.

References

Afflerbach, P. (2016). Reading assessment. *The Reading Teacher, 69*(4), 413–419.

Anderson, N. L., & Kaye, E. L. (2017). Finding versus fixing: Self-monitoring for readers who struggle. *The Reading Teacher, 70*(5), 543–550.

Arya, P., & Feathers, K. M. (2012). Reconsidering children's readings: Insights into the reading process. *Reading Psychology, 33*(4), 301–322. doi:10.1080/02702711.2010.51888

Clay, M. M. (1991). *Becoming literate: The construction of inner control.* Portsmouth, NH: Heinemann Educational Books.

Deno, S. L., Marston, D., Shinn, M. R., & Tindal, G. (1983). Oral reading fluency: A simple datum for scaling reading disability. *Topics in Learning and Learning Disabilities, 2*(4), 53–59.

Fountas, I. C., & Pinnell, G. S. (1996). *Guided reading: Good first teaching for all children.* Portsmouth, NH: Heinemann.

Goodman, K. (1996). *On reading.* Portsmouth, NH: Heinemann.

Goodman, Y. M., Watson, D. J., & Burke, C. L. (2005). *Reading miscue inventory: From evaluation to instruction* (2nd ed.). Katonah, NY: Richard C. Owen Publishers.

Hudson, R. F., Lane, H. B., & Pullen, P. C. (2005). Reading fluency assessment and instruction: What, why, and how? *The Reading Teacher, 58*(8), 702–714.

Kucer, S. B. (2014). What retellings can tell us about the nature of reading comprehension in school children. *Australian Journal of Language and Literacy, 37*(1), 31–44.

Liwanag, M. P. S. U., Martens, P., Martens, R., & Pelatti, C. Y. (2017a). Examining a reader's meaning-making process of picture books using eye movement miscue analysis. *Literacy Research: Theory, Method, and Practice, 66*(1), 248–263.

Liwanag, M. P. S. U., Martens, P., Martens, R. L., & Pelatti, C. Y. (2017b). Supporting multilingual learners as readers: Lessons from eye movement miscue analysis. *English Journal, 106*(3), 79–82.

Mantei, J., & Kervin, L. (2016). Tracking eye movements to gain insights into an older reader's reading practices. *Literacy Learning: The Middle Years, 24*(3), 36–44.

Paulson, E. J. (2002). Are oral reading word omissions and substitutions caused by careless eye movements? *Reading Psychology, 23*(1), 45–66.

Pillai, A. D. R., & Paramasivam, S. (2014). Miscue analysis of oral reading among non-proficient Malaysian ESL learners. *Journal of English Language and Literature, 2*(2), 179–185.

Rosenblatt, L. M. (1982). The literary transaction: Evocation and response. *Theory into Practice, 21*(4), 268–277.

Children's Literature Cited

Riddle, T. (2010). *My uncle's donkey.* Au: Penguin.

Watts, B. (2002). *Snake.* UK: Franklin Watts.

Note:

Images in Figures 4.1 and 4.2 include a reproduction of pp. 6–7 in Riddle, T. (2010). *My uncle's donkey.* Au: Penguin.

Images in Figures 4.3 and 4.4 include a reproduction of pp. 4–5 in Watts, B. (2002). *Snake.* UK: Franklin Watts.

5

Applying EMMA to Shared Reading in an Educational Setting With a Child With Special Needs

by Charlotte Clark, Ryan L. Nelson, Jack S. Damico, Holly L. Damico, Christine Weill, Laura E. Arrington, and Amanda Percle

The term "shared reading" has been used in a variety of ways to describe interactions between individuals of varying reading proficiency. It has been applied to successful remediation efforts of persons with specific language impairment (Damico, Abendroth, Nelson, Lynch & Damico, 2011; Damico, Damico, Nelson, Weill, & Maxwell, 2016; Damico & Nelson, 2010; Damico, Nelson, Damico, Abendroth, & Scott, 2008; Lynch, Damico, Nelson, & Abendroth, 2013; Nelson & Damico, 2006; Nelson, Damico, Smith, 2008; Nelson & Hawley, 2004). In these contexts, educators work to remediate, or achieve a therapeutic effect on the learner's proficiency. In our field of special education, a therapeutic effect is the impact an educator or clinician has on learners as they support the learners in becoming more proficient readers. Educators/clinicians have this impact by marshaling the collective approaches and strategies necessary to facilitate changes in the targeted areas of need for their readers.

The shared reading examined in this chapter is modeled after Routman (2003). Application of this model of shared reading to children with special needs occurs when an educator reads smoothly and with expression in a relaxed environment for the purpose of enjoying the passage. The child listens and is not quizzed or expected to retell or engage in formal comprehension assessments. During these interactions, the child sees the text and is invited to participate. A shared reading approach to literacy education allows the child opportunities for collaborative reading success. The child observes reading aloud by a more proficient reader and both transact with authentic text. When the child chooses to read, all of his efforts and approximations are valued by the educator. The goal is to create an overall positive and meaningful reading experience (Damico & Nelson, 2010).

How We Worked With Ronnie

Consistent with the theme of this book, we have used EMMA procedures for our primary data collection and analysis. In this chapter we focus on Catherine (the teacher) and Ronnie engaged in one of their routine one-on-one sessions. Twice weekly they worked together for an hour, focused on helping Ronnie develop language and literacy abilities needed for academic success. These sessions consisted of shared reading, writers workshop, and conversations about literacy.

Catherine holds a Ph.D. in speech-language pathology and works with children in a university clinic. She has over a decade of experience working with children similar to Ronnie. Ronnie is an 11-year-old fifth grade student and a monolingual English speaker from an upper-class, two-parent home. He carries multiple diagnoses intended to both account for the academic challenges he experiences and to qualify him for special services. Ronnie has been labeled with Specific Learning Disorder: impairment in reading and written expression, Spoken Language Disorder, and Attention Deficit Hyperactive Disorder (predominantly inattentive).

Upon meeting Ronnie, one quickly discovers his eagerness to please others and socialize in situations that do not require literacy. Like many children his age, he loves comic books, especially Marvel Superheroes. Ronnie recently traveled some distance with his friends and mother to attend a Fall Out Boy concert. His social strengths and interests create an initial impression that he is not one who has special needs. However, in the context of reading and academic tasks, his struggles quickly manifest themselves. Ronnie is reluctant to take risks and to trust his application of background knowledge while reading. He has difficulty integrating all language cueing systems when he reads, particularly with focusing on constructing meaning (semantic cueing system) when he reads.

Generally, children with diagnosed language disorders struggle with effectiveness, efficiency, and appropriateness of meaning-making (Damico, Müller, & Ball, 2010; Hamayan, Marler, López, & Damico, 2013). True to this description, Ronnie reads slowly and does not make sense in the manner accepted and valued by his school. These challenges with using language to make meaning qualified him to receive speech-language pathology services in a university clinic, which is how he and Catherine met. Catherine's work focused on helping Ronnie integrate all the cueing systems when he read. For four months, they worked together in 60-minute sessions twice a week. The sessions included conversation and literacy education in the contexts of writing workshop activities and shared reading.

Eye-Tracking Equipment and Software

We collected eye-tracking and scene/audio data using ASL's MobileEye, which samples at 60Hz and is accurate within one degree of the visual angle. Ronnie's right eye was tracked while he read aloud from *Mudshark* by Gary Paulsen (2009). Catherine selected this book as part of the services Ronnie was receiving. Ronnie and Catherine read a portion of this book in our eye-tracking lab to allow collection of Ronnie's visual sampling patterns during the shared reading portion of the session. We scanned pages from the book and displayed them on a computer monitor so that Catherine and Ronnie could both read off the screen at an angle required for accuracy in visual sampling calibration. We used ASL's MobileEye machine to collect data from Ronnie during the shared reading. The resulting fixation data were then analyzed on a fixation-by-fixation basis using default specifications of ASL ResultsPro analysis software. Additionally, we assigned codes to each fixation in order to classify and describe the patterns of fixation as they applied to reading. We achieved validity in coding through both calibration and synchronizing eye movement data with audio obtained through the scene camera.

EMMA Procedures

EMMA involves the integration of eye movement analysis with traditional Oral Reading Miscue Analysis. Because we were interested in studying shared reading, modifications to traditional Oral Reading Miscue Analysis (Goodman, Watson, & Burke, 2005) procedures had to occur. Additionally, the raw eye movement data had to be converted into audio data that could be matched in time with the production of Ronnie's oral reading miscues. We performed multiple analyses as part of the EMMA procedures. These analyses included an oral miscue analysis and a point-by-point analysis of Ronnie's visual sampling patterns. Our research team recorded, transcribed, and divided Ronnie and Catherine's shared reading session into 12 instances of reading during which Ronnie orally read from the text. We refer to these instances as Ronnie's "reading turns." Because his reading turns occurred in shared reading collaborations, Catherine monitored Ronnie's comprehension by attending to his miscues, oral reading efficiency, comments, and nonverbal reactions.

We examine Ronnie's miscue patterns in light of our fixation-by-fixation analysis in our results section that follows. In order to interpret his eye movements in relation to his miscues, we manually reviewed and applied descriptive codes to Ronnie's visual fixations in chronological sequence, applying five different codes to describe each fixation. These data were derived from automatically generated ASL Results Plus fixation data. We developed and applied codes by addressing the following:

1. Was the fixation on a word?

2. Considering fixation sequence, did the fixation constitute progressive or regressive eye movement? When a fixation was observed moving from left-to-right, a code of "forward" was applied. Movements from right-to-left were coded as "regressive."

3. What was the fixated word? How did the fixated word corresponded to the timing of Ronnie's oral reading?

4. Often readers fixate in the white spaces between lines and in margins. For fixations that did not occur directly on a word, we asked if the fixation was within a foveal window of 3–6 letters of the target line. In doing so, fixations in the white spaces were assigned to words in the same manner as has been described in the literature referencing target word identification (Rayner, 1998; Rayner, Yang, Schuett, & Slattery, 2013).

5. Are decisions of coding accuracy verifiable? This was determined by periodically matching Ronnie's voice with the line being read and monitoring the fixation transitions at the end of every line (e.g., return sweeps). Though not observed in this study, if mismatch occurred, recalibration would be needed.

Two researchers completed the coding process and any disagreements concerning the coding of specific fixations were deliberated until they reached consensus. In order to determine the reliability of coding, approximately 10% of the fixation codes and miscues were evaluated by two EMMA trained researchers employed at universities not participating in this study. No instances of coding inaccuracy were identified.

Our analysis yielded a representation of Ronnie's visual patterns from which we calculated how many of his fixations were progressive versus regressive movements. We also analyzed the average fixation duration with significant attention to the average duration of regressions. Because regressions typically reflect instances of potential interest (Just & Carpenter, 1987; Rayner, 2009; Rayner, Chace, Slattery, & Ashby, 2006) we also calculated the percentage of fixation regressions and percentage of within word regressions. These data allowed consideration of how Ronnie's visual pattern triangulated with our marked typescript of the oral miscues he produced during the shared-oral reading and our fine-grain analysis of visual patterns during moments of mediation. Due to limitations of space, we identified a typical example from one of Ronnie's reading turns and share a fine-grain analysis of this, his 11th out of 12 turns at reading, for an illustration of the application of eye-tracking technology to shared-reading events.

Finally, to verify our findings we followed procedures consistent with qualitative research (Nelson & Damico, 2006). After the session, we interviewed Catherine and asked her to reflect on instances where she provided mediation. She described her decision-making process at specific instances. We transcribed her impressions of both Ronnie's reading turns and her own mediation to consider them in relation to Ronnie's oral miscues and his visual patterns. We use these perceptions for verification of our observations from analysis of the eye movement data and miscue data. For the purposes of this chapter, we weave Catherine's interview data for reflective impressions of Ronnie's 11th reading turn with the illustrative results presented.

What We Learned

In order to consider EMMA's contributions to the understanding of how shared reading benefits the development of children with diagnosis of specific language impairment, results of the data sources must be overlaid. In this section, we describe the results of our various layers of analysis. We first present a general description of the overall observed mediation in the shared reading session, followed by a brief description of the analysis of Ronnie's miscues. We present these descriptions to illustrate the context, strategies, and focused transactions Ronnie and Catherine used. We then present the eye movement data in terms of Ronnie's overall visual sampling across all of the reading turns, followed by EMMA results drawing from all of the analyzed data in a specific interactional sequence (e.g., reading turn 11).

Overall Observed Mediation in Shared Reading

During Catherine and Ronnie's shared reading session, Ronnie experienced opportunities to make sense of the text on his own; however, when Catherine recognized he was struggling, she meditated in multiple ways. She strategically identified and read significant portions of the text, demonstrating proficient reading and frequently verbalizing the "readerly choices" (Johnston, 2004) she was making. She worked to ensure that his understanding of the story was sufficient enough to allow him to draw from appropriate sources and read with balanced integration of the language cueing systems. In addition, Catherine often summarized parts of the text before extending a reading turn to Ronnie. Based upon her relationship with Ronnie, she strategically posed rhetorical and actual questions inviting him to relate his own personal experience and background knowledge to portions of the texts. She encouraged Ronnie's predictions of both future events in the story or the actions characters might take.

Together they discussed relevant portions of text as they encountered them. Some of these mediational tactics are observed in the illustrative presentation associated with Ronnie's 11th reading turn. All of Catherine's mediation was provided as part of a natural, conversation-like, interactive style that arose as the two collaboratively navigated the story.

Analysis of Oral Miscues

The overall aim of this chapter is to consider how eye movement data informs the understanding of shared reading instruction's collaborative transactions. To assist in meeting this aim, we used miscue analysis to analyze Ronnie's reading attempts during the shared session. His oral reading productions offer insight into his efforts to make sense of print. Because the interactions between Ronnie and Catherine were instructional, Catherine actively monitored Ronnie's comprehension by discussing the story and possible meanings during the shared reading and did not collect a formal retelling at the end. In addition, her real time interpretations of Ronnie's comprehension drove her mediational decisions.

A general overview of Ronnie's miscues produced during his 12 reading turns across this session provide insight into how he weaves cueing systems together when reading. Within these reading turns, he read 386 words, miscuing on 36 words, or 9.32% of the text. Ronnie self-corrected 4.80% of his miscues, primarily through multiple attempts at sounding out words he knew didn't make sense. His low quality miscues, characterized by substitutions with a high degree of graphophonic similarity, accounted for 3.01% of the text. We contextualize the miscue patterns at specific points of mediation in the transactions of shared reading with the eye movement data below.

Visual Patterns Across Reading Turns

We confined our analysis of eye-movement data to moments immediately surrounding Ronnie's reading turns. Each reading turn required unique transactional strategies. This resulted in a range of variation in data points produced from each specific reading turn. Table 5.1 reflects these differences. The first two columns of this table show the number of words associated with each of Ronnie's reading turns. Subsequent columns display the time and fixation data generated as he completed the various reading turns. Data points with notably large variability include the number of words read per reading turn (i.e., range of 9–94 words), the associated number of fixations (i.e., range of 30–220 fixations per reading turn) and Ronnie's reading rate (i.e., range of 38.96–94.57 prorated words read per minute).

Additionally, the duration of fixations on text read in each turn also varied from an average fixation duration of 0.259–0.347 seconds. Each reading turn contained regressive fixations. The average number of regressive fixations per turn at reading ranged between 9.01–28.26% of the total fixations. When examining authentic reading behaviors, Ronnie's regressive fixations occurred within the same word and extended across both word and sentence boundaries. Consistent with Ronnie's challenges with integrating the semantic cueing system, a substantial portion of his regressive fixations occurred as he prioritized his visual sampling to word-centric analysis while reading. This pattern of reliance on graphophonic input is supported by the range of within word regressive fixations across all reading turns (i.e., 42.9–86.67% within word regressions).

These overall descriptions of observed interactional patterns and reading behaviors form the foundational eye movement data necessary for EMMA analysis into how shared reading supports a child with special needs. We will

Reading Turns	Words Read	Words per minute	Fixations	Average Fixation Duration	% of Regressive Fixation	Average Regression Duration	% of Within Word Regressions
1	20	76.09	46	.266	28.26	.273	69.23
2	23	77.4	52	.259	23.08	.238	58.33
3	22	53.64	63	.302	23.81	.282	86.67
4	36	77.95	81	.266	17.28	.251	64.29
5	36	70.47	84	.284	16.67	.264	42.9
6	36	61.79	97	.288	20.62	.326	75
7	31	74.16	68	.272	19.12	.29	69.23
8	15	73.59	33	.292	9.01	.323	66.67
9	29	94.57	52	.29	17.31	.227	55.56
10	9	38.96	30	.347	23.33	.241	42.86
11	35	62.19	86	.319	18.6	.383	56.25
12	94	72.11	220	.274	15.91	.221	57.14

Table 5.1: Visual Sampling Data for Each of Ronnie's Reading Turns
Source: Authors.

now turn to how EMMA informs our understanding of shared reading by illustrating a closer analysis of these same variables during one of Ronnie's reading turns.

Fine Grain EMMA Analysis at Moment of Mediation in Turn 11

We chose a specific moment of mediation on which to perform closer analysis, utilizing eye-tracking technology as a way of exploring Ronnie's visual behaviors in relation to Catherine's mediation strategies during his 11th reading turn. Similar analysis could focus on mediation during any of the reading turns. At this point in the story a quirky librarian, Mrs. Underdorf, was wondering why her new pet armadillo, Sparky, had not moved in its cage. The main character Lyle, who is also nicknamed "Mudshark," is with Mrs. Underdorf and begins to poke around in the armadillo's terrarium. On the left in Table 5.2, we display the six lines of text we selected for closer analysis. On the right is the transcript of the shared reading. The duration and sequential production of fixations associated with Ronnie's visual inspection of Line 3 and Line 4 are shown in Table 5.3. Ideally, we would create an image that affixes the fixations to the text. However, due to the dynamic nature of recording with our MobilEye, we are not able to do that. This is a major limitation of our system for demonstration purposes such as this.

Of particular interest is Catherine's choice to take over the reading responsibility from Ronnie at the midpoint of this paragraph (Line 5). This interactional shift occurred even though Ronnie had just made a self-correction (Line 4: "'Well, I'll be . . .' sh— . . .'Well, I'll be,' she said"), adding the appropriate prosody and self-correcting "sh—" to "she said." However, Catherine was cued into Ronnie's behaviors prior to this partial miscue.

Text from *Mudshark* by Gary Paulsen		Transcript from Ronnie's Oral Reading
1.　Ms. Underdorf peered intently at Spark. Mud- 2. shark's nudge had flipped him on his side and out of 3. the burrows of wood shavings. 4.　"Well, I'll be...," she said. "Would you look at 5. that! It's a purse! Sparky is actually a purse. Fine obser- 6. vation, Lyle." She beamed proudly at Mudshark.	R (reading)	1. Ms. Underdorf peered in-intently at Sparky, 2. Mudshark nudged (huh exhalation) had flipped him 　　on his side and out of 3. the burrow of wood...shavings. 4. Well I 'll be sh well I'll be she said. Would you look 　　at that? 5. It's a purse.
	R (comment)	Oh my gosh/
	C (reading)	5. (laughs) Sparky is actually a purse! Fine 6.　observation, Lyle
	C (comment)	which is Mudshark's real name, huh?/

Table 5.2: Lines of Text and Ronnie's Oral Productions

Source: Paulsen, G. (2009, p. 23). *Mudshark*. New York: Wendy Lamb Books.
Source: Authors.

The importance of considering the broader influence on Catherine's decision making becomes apparent through the EMMA lens. Ronnie's low-quality miscue in Line 1, his attempt to sound out "intently," reflected a reliance on graphophonic cues. His visual sampling at this same time included a total of seven fixations on this word, two of which were regressions. In Line 2, he omitted the possessive on "Mudshark's," fixating on it only once for 0.33 seconds. He then added the regular past tense marker "-ed" to "nudge" (producing "nudged"), while fixating on this word four times for a total visual inspection duration of 1.78 seconds. It is likely his omission of the possessive in "Mudshark's" led to a predicted expectation that "nudge" should, in Ronnie's mind, be one of matching tense. Ronnie's syntactic knowledge influenced his insertion of the past tense "-ed" to make sense of the text. When these changes to the text no longer met his syntactic or semantic expectations, he increased his visual input as seen by the 1.78 second overall fixation on "nudge" prior to producing the miscue, "nudged." From this point, Ronnie's reading intonation became slower and choppier, nevertheless he kept moving forward in the text without overtly (i.e., verbal production or visual inspection) correcting the oral miscues.

In Line 3, he produced a notable pause between "wood" and "shavings," with his intonation on wood consistent with a sentence break (see Table 5.3). Visual data supports this interpretation as he fixated on each of the final four words in the line three times. The total visual inspection time of "burrow," "of," and "wood" were 0.8s, 0.53s, and 0.61s, respectively. However, in support of the oral miscue driven interpretation that Ronnie expected the sentence to end with "wood," he produced his longest total fixation duration in Line 3 when he fixated on "shavings" for 1.44 seconds. His next fixations took him to Line 4 as he began the next paragraph.

In line 4, Ronnie began the oral reading of "'Well, I'll be,' sh— . . ." with a slow, choppy, word-by-word approach. He produced "sh—" and paused while fixating on " . . .". His eye movement data at this point shows he fixated on "Well" four times for a total fixation duration time of 0.7 seconds. His next

Line 3	Total Fixation Durations				.8s	.53s	.61s		1.44s	
	Fixation Order				2 1 3	4 5 6	7 8 9		10 12 11	
	Printed Text			the	burrows	of	wood		shavings.	
	Ronnie's reading			"the burrow of wood (pause) shavings"						
Line 4	Total Fixation Durations	.7s	.24s.		.67s	.46s	.87s	1.72s.		.14s
	Fixation Order	1 2 3 4	5		6	7 8	11 13	9 10 12 14 15 16 17		18
	Printed Text	"Well	I'll	be	...,"	she	said	Would	you	look	at
	Ronnie's reading	"Well I'll be sh well I'll be she said. Would you look at"								

Table 5.3: The Duration and Sequential Production of Fixations Associated With Ronnie's Visual Inspection

Source: Paulsen, G. (2009, p. 23). *Mudshark*. New York: Wendy Lamb Books.
Source: Authors.

fixation was a brief 0.24 seconds on "I'll," followed by a single somewhat longer fixation on " . . ." of 0.67 seconds. At this point, Ronnie corrects the "sh—" and intonation when he reads "'Well, I'll be,' she said." Data in Table 5.3 explicate Ronnie's second, revising attempt at Line 4. He does not visually regress to "Well, I'll be"; rather, he visually inspects the words "she," "said," and "would" through a series of progressions and two regressive fixations. His total fixation duration on the words "said" and "would" of 0.87s and 1.72s respectively indicate that the revisions he was making were occurring primarily in his mind based upon the mental text constructed on his first pass. He then read without miscue to the midpoint of Line 5, where the big reveal in the story is made. Seemingly having understood that Mrs. Underdorf's pet armadillo was not really an armadillo, Ronnie looked to share this moment of surprise with Catherine and gasped, "Oh my gosh!" (See Table 5.2, Line 5).

While Ronnie read by Line 4 and appeared to comprehend the big surprise of the story in Line 5, his visual sampling patterns combined with the cumulative effect of his miscues suggest that he was still having to work to make sense of the text. Catherine decided to carry on reading the rest of Line 5 and Line 6 herself. The cumulative effect of Ronnie's miscues and the extended fixation duration times at areas of miscue, as well as his preference for resolving miscues through within word regressions suggest he was not efficient in his visual sampling. Our data for Ronnie's visual sampling during reading turn 11, found in Table 5.3, reveal that he made nine within word regressions out of 16 regressions in total. In relation to his oral reading miscues, the timing and prevalence of regressions and the within word nature of Ronnie's fixations are consistent with research indicating readers launch regressive fixations at moments of linguistic confusion (Just & Carpenter, 1987; Rayner et al., 2006). These visual patterns better illuminate the meaning-making context leading up to Catherine's decision to provide mediation.

Data from the interview with Catherine, collected after the session, show her insightful mediational decision making. For example, her description of mediation associated with Line 5 came without knowledge of the eye movement data or a transcript of Ronnie's miscues. She explained:

> Mhm, well, it started when he lost this punctuation, but he seemed to do okay with that because losing the possessive on "Mudshark's nudge" changed it to "Mudshark nudged had flipped." And so I was afraid right there that we were already starting to lose who was doing what and what was flipping, right? . . . I kind of let him go. I said, "Okay . . . Let's see if he picks up that it's a purse . . . Here he kind of read it flat, but then he went back and re-read it a little better. But I just felt like he was hanging on by sort of a thin thread there, and that if I didn't get in . . . he would start to just read these as narrative sentences rather than as a continual, you know, the teacher continuing to talk to Mudshark about the purse.

Despite his self-correction and change in intonation just prior to her mediation, Ronnie's overall turn percentage of within-word regressions, combined with his oral miscues, suggest he was having trouble making sense of the story and was limiting his visual sampling to integration of graphophonic cue. This assessment fits with Catherine's impressions of Ronnie's reading at this point. The cumulative effect of Ronnie's transactions with print led Catherine to believe her mediation was necessary to either solidify or reestablish understanding of what was happening in the story. EMMA data support the appropriateness of her mediational timing and approach.

Discussion

EMMA findings applied to shared reading in this student lend support to educators oriented to appreciation of miscues and the importance of viewing reading as a meaningful transaction with text. By manually coding Ronnie's visual fixations in a chronological sequence, we constructed a transcript of his visual patterns and considered them in light of his oral miscues and Catherine's mediation. Our fine grain analysis of a specific moment of mediation, when Catherine decided to intervene and began reading the text herself, aligned with instructional impressions of Ronnie's reading process up to that moment. By listening to him read Catherine was able to successfully judge the amount of effort Ronnie had to exert in order to continue making sense. Even though his voice regained a natural intonation and he did not miscue in Line 5, our analysis of his visual sampling suggested that Ronnie was still laboring in his transactions with print. EMMA revealed parts of the reading process that were invisible to Catherine during shared reading, and in this instance, confirmed her impressions of Ronnie. Given Ronnie's prior miscues, his lack of smooth and fluid reading earlier in the passage, and the nature of the punctuation in the text, Catherine decided that she should intervene in order to support Ronnie's continued meaning-making in his next reading turn.

This study points to the future research potential of applications of EMMA to shared-reading events. With EMMA, researchers can examine the choices reading educators make in light of a child's visual sampling patterns. Likewise, a child's visual inspection of the text can be examined in light of an educator's choices in mediation. There is a tie that binds an educator and child with each other during shared reading. This study reveals some of the threads forming this connection. Successful reading mediation is based upon a responsive relationship rather than prescribed interactional sequences. Such relationships require a level of attunement between reading partners, as shown here between Catherine and Ronnie. EMMA provides another way to measure, describe and interpret this attunement, both what makes it successful and what gets in the way. Such insight is valuable for any professional who works in the realm of language and literacy.

References

Damico, J. S., Abendroth, K., Nelson, R. L., Lynch, K. E., & Damico, H. L. (2011). Research report: Variations on the theme of avoidance as compensations during unsuccessful reading performance. *Clinical Linguistics and Phonetics, 25,* 741–752.

Damico, J., Damico, H., Nelson, R., Weill, C., & Maxwell, J. (2016). Infusing meaning and joy back into books: Reclaiming literacy in young children with autism spectrum disorders. In R. Meyer & K. Whitmore (Eds.), *Reclaiming early childhood literacies: Narratives of hope, power, and vision* (pp. 109–119). New York, NY: Routledge.

Damico, J. S., Müller, N., & Ball, M. J. (2010). Social and practical considerations in labeling. In J. S. Damico, N. Müller & M. J. Ball (Eds.), *The handbook of language and speech disorders* (pp.11–37). Malden, MA: Wiley-Blackwell.

Damico, J. S., & Nelson, R. (2010). Reading and reading impairments. In J. S. Damico, N. Müller, & M. J. Ball (Eds.), *The handbook of language and speech disorders* (pp 267–295). Malden, MA: Wiley-Blackwell.

Damico, J., Nelson, R., Damico, H., Abendroth, K., & Scott, J. (2008). Avoidance strategies in an exceptional child during unsuccessful reading performances. *Clinical Linguistics and Phonetics, 22,* 283–291.

Goodman, Y., Watson, D., & Burke, C. (2005). *Reading miscue inventory: From evaluation to instruction.* Katonah, NY: Richard C. Owen Publishers, Inc.

Hamayan, E. V., Marler, B., López, C. S., & Damico, J. (2013). *Special education considerations for English language learners: Delivering a continuum of services.* Philadelphia: Caslon Publishing.

Johnston, P. H. (2004). *Choice words: How our language affects children's learning.* Portland, ME: Stenhouse Publishing.

Just, M., & Carpenter, P. (1987). *The psychology of reading and language comprehension.* Newton, MA: Allyn and Bacon.

Lynch, K. E., Damico, J. S., Nelson, R. L., & Abendroth, K. (2013). Reading performance subsequent to aphasia: Strategies applied during authentic reading. *Aphasiology, 27,* 723–739.

Nelson, R., & Damico, J. S. (2006). Qualitative research in literacy acquisition: A framework for investigating reading in children with language impairment. *Clinical Linguistics and Phonetics, 20,* 631–639.

Nelson, R., Damico, J., & Smith, S. (2008). Applying eye movement miscue analysis to the reading patterns of children with language impairment. *Clinical Linguistics and Phonetics, 22,* 293–303.

Nelson, R., & Hawley, H. (2004). Inner control as an operational mechanism in attention deficit hyperactivity disorder. *Seminars in Speech and Language, 25,* 255–261.

Paulsen, G. (2009). *Mudshark.* New York: Wendy Lamb Books.

Rayner, K. (1998). Eye movements in reading and information processing: 20 years of research. *Psychological Bulletin, 124*(3), 372–422.

Rayner, K. (2009). Eye movements and attention in reading, scene perception, and visual search. *Quarterly Journal of Experimental Psychology, 62,* 1547–1506.

Rayner, K., Chace, K.H., Slattery, T. J., & Ashby, J. (2006). Eye movements as reflections of comprehension processes in reading. *Scientific Studies of Reading, 10,* 241–255.

Rayner, K, Yang, J., Schuett, S., & Slattery, T. J. (2013). Eye movements of older and younger readers when reading unspaced text. *Experimental Psychology, 60,* 354–361.

Routman, R. (2003). *Reading essentials: The specifics you need to teach reading well.* Portsmouth, NH: Heinemann.

6

"Feelings of Uncertainty and Certainty"

An Exploration of an Emergent Doctoral Researcher Through a Collaborative EMMA Inquiry

by Honor B. McElroy, Judith K. Franzak, Heather D. Porter, and Koomi J. Kim

In this chapter, we focus on our processes as a collaborative research team in mentoring a new doctoral student in her development as an eye movement miscue analysis (EMMA) researcher. Our team included three faculty mentors (Koomi, Judi, and Heather) and one doctoral student (Honor). The collaborative and dialogic nature of this team—with a diverse range of professional and research backgrounds including early, adolescent, and adult literacy—illustrates the potential for EMMA research to be a powerful tool for doctoral students to understand and apply to their professional context. Our inquiry was guided by the following question: What insights does an emergent EMMA researcher, who is also a secondary English language arts teacher, develop through an EMMA experience as part of a collaborative inquiry?

Background of Eye Movement Miscue Research

EMMA is theoretically grounded in the sociopsycholinguistic transactional model of reading, which recognizes readers as active meaning makers in the process of comprehending texts. Furthermore, this model illuminates how readers' integration of knowledge and strategies act to guide and support how they make sense of what they read (K. Goodman, Fries, & Strauss, 2016). As readers read texts, their perceptual activity is informed and driven by their sociocognitive knowledge of language and reading strategies in an effort to construct a parallel model of the text. EMMA research demonstrates how proficient readers draw upon their own knowledge and the author's text to transact meaning as they continuously sample, make predictions, monitor their understanding, and confirm their inferences as they read. Reading is a dynamic, constructive process of making meaning (K. Goodman et al., 2016).

As a research method, EMMA combines two distinct forms of inquiry: miscue analysis—involving the examination of differences between readers' observed responses and the expected responses in the text—and the exploration of readers' visual eye movements during their oral reading of a text (K. Goodman et al., 2016). By integrating this data, researchers study what types of miscues happen during reading (e.g., omissions, substitutions, regressions) and compare those to camera generated snapshots of what the eye does during the miscues. This combination provides a means of accessing readers' moment-to-moment comprehending processes. As part of this process, identified miscues are analyzed to understand how readers draw upon their existing graphophonic, semantic, and syntactic knowledge as well as schema to make sense of written text (K. Goodman et al., 2016). Some questions that EMMA researchers pose are: *Do the miscues make sense? Do the miscues sound like a language? Do the miscues change meaning?* (Y. Goodman, Watson, & Burke, 2005, p. 104). Researchers combine this information with the visual map of the reader's continuous eye movements generated during the oral reading to elicit a deeper understanding of the relationship between readers' perceptual input of text and sociocognitive transactions of meaning. In this step of the analysis, researchers ask: *What is the nature of their eye fixations as they read? What patterns of eye movements emerge (i.e., regressions, fixation durations, and flow of reading)? How do these patterns support an understanding of readers' observed miscues?* (Paulson, 2002).

By integrating both lines of inquiry into one methodology, EMMA offers a holistic understanding of reading in relation to readers' perceptual movements and comprehending processes, thereby further revealing the centrality of readers as meaning makers (Paulson, Flurkey, Goodman, & Goodman, 2003). While prior research demonstrates the efficacy of this method for understanding the universal processes all readers engage in during reading (K. Goodman et al., 2016), the goal of this study is to describe the insights an emergent graduate researcher gains from a collaborative EMMA inquiry project regarding her own understanding of reading processes, inquiry, and pedagogy.

Research Background

Honor was a first-year doctoral student and graduate research assistant in the program in which Koomi, Judi, and Heather taught. As a team we gathered data at the Salisbury University EMMA lab. Honor's interest in the pedagogy of reading stemmed from her interdisciplinary and disciplinary work as a high school educator. She began her career as an English teacher and interdisciplinary leader at a public high school in a rural Appalachian county, which was part of the Qualla Boundary for the Eastern Band of Cherokee Indians. One initiative in which Honor was involved was an interdisciplinary redesign of curriculum to better support the perceived needs of students identified as at risk for not completing high school as indicated by standardized and school assessment data. When the program was cut due to budget constraints, Honor sought a new experience within a different educational context. Thus, she taught in international high schools in the Dominican Republic and Jordan for seven years, focusing on English studies, curriculum redesign, collaboration, and multilingualism. Honor has always had a keen interest in language and has both formal and informal educational experiences learning Spanish. At the time of this study she was pursuing her doctoral degree to investigate the reading processes and experiences of adolescent and adult readers.

Honor was drawn to EMMA because of the potential she saw in it for complementing the pedagogy of strategic reading as both a literacy intervention for adolescent learners (Baye, Inns, Lake, & Slavin, 2018; Reynolds, 2020) and as the basis for pedagogy in the English language arts classroom (e.g., Beers, 2004). Across her career, Honor found that she struggled with eliciting information about sociocognitive processes that her students utilized and saw EMMA as a powerful tool to potentially address this aspect of her teaching.

During this semester long study, the team worked with Honor to conduct observations of building and conducting an eye tracker experiment. As part of this process Honor assisted with the development of a procedural manual for using the eye tracker software and participated in the department-wide study group's training sessions that covered data gathering and data analysis procedures using SR Research (2017) desktop eye tracker, EyeLink 1000 Plus, and Data Viewer software. She also built her own knowledge through a literature review of foundational work in EMMA research.

How We Gathered EMMA Data for This Study

In order to help Honor learn about EMMA research, we conducted a collaborative inquiry project involving one EMMA session, lasting 60 minutes, in which Honor read aloud the folktale, "The Man Who Kept House" (McInnes, 1962). This folktale has 711 words and is often used for instructional purposes in addition to helping researchers and teachers develop strategies for miscue analysis (Fries, 2008; Y. Goodman et al., 2005). For that reason, we chose this text as a way for Honor to experience the EMMA process through her own inquiry as an adult reader. Following her oral reading, Honor recounted her understanding through unaided and aided retelling sessions with Heather and Koomi. Both the oral reading and retelling sessions were audio-recorded for analysis and the EyeLink 1000 Plus was used to track and record her eye movements.

Following the EMMA data gathering session, Honor listened to the audio-recording of her reading and marked her miscues on a typescript of the story (Y. Goodman et al., 2005). Koomi separately listened and marked Honor's miscues in order to ensure inter-rater reliability. This process included several discussions between Koomi and Honor in which Honor demonstrated increasing proficiency in using miscue analysis. Our team decided to focus specifically on marking as an important first step for Honor to learn about miscue analysis and eye movement study. The marked typescript provided an opportunity for Honor to identify areas of interest for further reflection.

Honor also transcribed her aided and unaided retellings. In her research memos, she compared the aided and unaided retellings to the marked typescript of her miscues in order to observe and document insights about her reading comprehending and comprehension processes. Honor observed video recordings of her eye movement patterns as well as audio recordings of her oral reading to examine the relationship between her eye movements and miscued areas of the text. In the section that follows, we present three areas of interest (AOIs) to highlight Honor's reflections and learning processes as an emerging EMMA researcher.

Reflecting and Making Sense of EMMA Data

Reflection on the First Area of Interest

Honor's self-reflection on each area of interest highlights connections between her meaning-making processes across the individual miscue samples and the whole text (Porter, Kim, Franzak, & MacDonald, 2020). For example, Figure

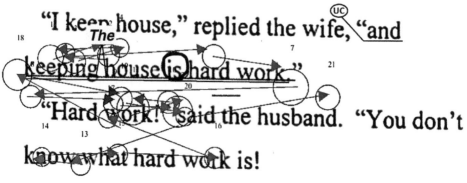

Figure 6.1: Honor's Eye Movements During Her Miscue of "Keeping House"

Note: The numbers correspond to the fixation points.
Source: Authors.
Source: McInnes, J. (1962, p. 282). *The man who kept house*. New York: Abelard-Schumann.

6.1 illustrates her dynamic nonlinear sampling process as she made two observed responses (miscues) while reading the text:

Text: . . . keeping house is hard work.

Honor: . . . keeping *the* house hard work. Hard—and keeping *the* house is hard work.

Figure 6.1 demonstrates Honor's nonlinear eye movements as she read the text, revealing how she did not fixate on every word she read. She fixated on the content words more frequently than she did on the function words. The multiple saccades between fixation points 1 and 5 demonstrate how Honor's eyes were regressing within the phrase "keeping house." Honor reflected on her own eye movement pattern:

> . . . my eye movement shows how I regressed to two words "keeping house" after I omitted the word "is" in the clause "keeping house is." This regression marks efficient movement to the beginning of my self-correction. It illustrates the process of how I was disconfirming my initial prediction of not including the verb "is," then I decided to regress to correct the omission of the verb "is."

Also, Honor reflected on how she was integrating the language cueing systems regarding this area of interest:

> When analyzing Figure 6.1, I noticed that my eyes did not fixate on the verb "is" in my initial reading of text. I did not sample this word. However, during my regression, my fixation points 10 through 12 indicate that I fixated on the word "is," regressed, and then fixate on "is" again in order to correct my miscue. K. Goodman et al. (2016) provide a description of the linguistic foundations for cueing systems that informs my understanding of language cueing systems operating at three levels: graphophonic (visual look), syntactic (structure), and semantic (meaning). In this case, I used semantic and syntactic knowledge to disconfirm the omission of the verb from the sentence and then regressed to correct the sentence.

Across both of these insights, Honor effectively drew upon and integrated her analysis of the observed miscues with the eye patterns to inform her understanding of how her perceptual activity was guided by her knowledge of the language cueing systems and her active monitoring of her comprehension.

In addition, Honor noted how she inserted "the" before house, yet when she regressed to self-correct her omission "is," she repeated her insertion of the determiner "the" before "house." Here is how Honor described her insertion miscue "the":

> This idiomatic phrase is not part of my linguistic and cultural repertoire and feels uncomfortable to say. I would say "clean the house." Thus, while the insertion of "the" follows the pattern of conventional syntactic rules, it also follows my own patterns

of language use. Once again, I used my syntactic and semantic knowledge to actively construct meaning from the text.

Honor's analysis illustrates how she was developing a deeper awareness and understanding of how she was using the language cueing systems and cognitive reading strategies while she was self-correcting the miscue, which did not make sense to her.

Reflection on the Second Area of Interest

The second area of interest shows similar patterns in the integration of sociocognitive strategies and language cueing systems as Honor made two high quality miscues. As Figure 6.2 shows, her first miscue was to substitute "came" for "cam," which was an existing typo in the original text. Although Honor did not notice the typo as she read, our team identified it through our discussion of the second miscue Honor made within this area of interest. Honor substituted the word "home" for the phrase "near the house" and then regressed to the beginning of the sentence to self-correct.

> Text: As she cam near the house . . .

> Honor: As she came home, as she came near the house . . .

In this miscue, Honor substitutues "home" for "house." She then regresses, repeats "as she came," and self corrects by adding "near the house." This miscue demonstrates another example of Honor's dynamic process as illustrated by the nonlinear eye movement pattern in the area surrounding the miscue, fixation points 4 through 14 (see Figure 6.2). Honor described her reading as:

> I again read efficiently by regressing [see fixation points 10 through 12] to the exact fixation point of the substitution miscue "home" for "house." While "home" and

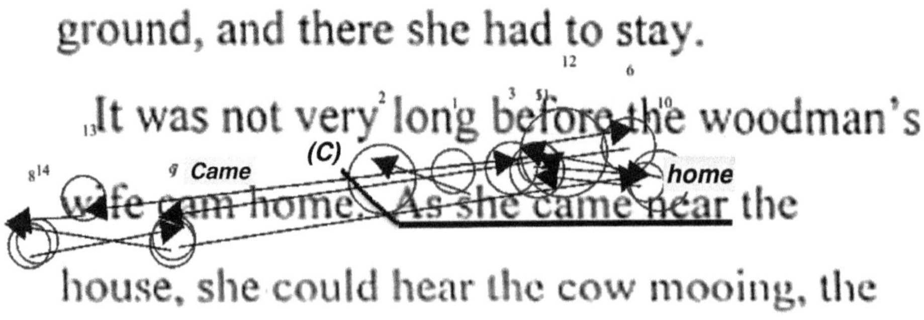

Figure 6.2: Honor's Eye Movements During Her Substitution Miscue

Source: Authors.
Source: McInnes, J. (1962, p. 284). *The man who kept house*. New York: Abelard-Schumann.

"house" look similar, I disconfirmed the substitution of "home" for a prepositional phrase ending with "house" using my syntactic cueing system. The efficiency in this miscue highlights the precision of my sampling and confirming as I stop and regress within this phrase.

Honor predicted "home" at first, but her eye movement revealed how she decided to disconfirm her prediction of "home" by self-correcting it to "house" as soon as she saw the phrase "near the house." However, her initial interpretation of her area of interest is still word-centric based on her understanding of the graphophonic cueing system. In this instance, Honor overlooked her sophisticated, nonlinear eye movements and her sociocognitive strategies that she subconsciously used in favor of this word-centric, graphophonic analysis. In our group discussion, Honor was surprised by the nuances that can be parced out through a comprehensive analysis of miscues and eye movements. Specifically, Honor realized that the cueing systems work together and miscues cannot really be attributed to one system. Her prediction of "home," for example, wasn't based solely on graphophonics but included her syntactic and semantic knowledge of the story. This examination shows Honor's initial exploration of her processes and developing knowledge of the language cueing systems.

Reflection on the Third Area of Interest
In the third area of interest (see Figure 6.3) Honor identified how she drew upon syntactic, semantic, and graphophonic language cues when she substituted "dishes" for "clothes."

> Text: "If you stay home to do my work you'll have to make butter, carry water from the well, wash the clothes, clean the house, and look after the baby," said the wife.

> Honor: "If you stay home to do my work, you'll have to make butter, carry water from the well, wash the *dishes*, clean the house, and look after the baby," said the wife.

Here is Honor's interpretation of her substitution miscue:

> I repeated the pattern of using my semantic and syntactic knowledge to confirm the acceptability of the substitution of a noun for a noun. In addition, this substitution has partial acceptability in terms of semantic acceptability and some graphophonic similarity. My eyes did not regress. Possible reasons for my substitution show similar patterns to my insertion of "the" in area of interest 1. In my own linguistic repertoire, I would say "do the laundry" not "wash the clothes." However, I would say "wash the dishes." Thus my own schema and linguistic patterns shape the text that I construct from this written text.

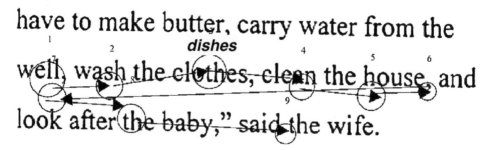

Figure 6.3: Honor's Eye Movements During Her Substitution Miscue of "Dishes"

Source: Authors.
Source: McInnes, J. (1962, p. 282). *The man who kept house*. New York: Abelard-Schumann.

Honor's substitution miscue partially affected the meaning of the text. Also, Honor noted that she did not regress or self-correct the miscue in relation to her eye movement and miscue analysis data. As it was the case for this miscue, Honor substituted "dishes" for "clothes." Her substitution miscue had some graphic similarity, as the ending morphemes match, but did not have sound similarity. Often, a low-quality miscue can have a high graphophonic similarity due to overreliance on the graphophonic cueing system. Through the discussion of this particular area of interest, Honor began to understand the acceptability of readers' miscues in relation to their interpretations of texts.

Reading Comprehension: Aided and Unaided Retelling

After Honor finished reading the folktale, the team asked her to retell the story. Here is how Honor recounted her unaided and aided retellings:

> My first purpose in reflecting on my retelling was to evaluate my comprehension of the entire text. I was able to summarize the key points of the folktale: the woodman's skepticism about the difficulty of his wife's work, their job reversal, and the woodman's inability to complete the wife's work. I also pointed out parts of the text that confused me: I stated that the rope was tied to the woodman's leg, but then I trailed off, saying, "Or someone's leg."
> Koomi's subsequent transition into an aided retelling prompted me to talk about the end of the story. At this point, I discussed the wife's ultimate rescue of her family as well as the cow and the fact that the woodman and his wife did not reverse jobs again. Koomi asked why the cow was on the roof. While I identified safety as the reason for the cow being on the roof, I did not talk about the fact that the cow was also on the roof to eat grass, which was a detail I did not recall.

Even when rereading the folktale for data analysis, the idea of putting a cow on a roof to eat confounded Honor. In our discussions, we prompted Honor to unpack her prior knowledge in relation to this image. Through her reflection, she realized the importance of her schema in transacting with the text and further recognized how her miscues were socioculturally constructed. Thus, the aided and unaided retelling offered Honor an important opportunity to understand, not just the comprehension of a text, but also the schematic knowledge that readers use when transacting with the text.

Final Reflections

In reflecting on Honor's experiences with EMMA and our ongoing work, we recognize the importance of sustaining dialogic exchange in supporting our collective learning. Several insights emerged from our conversations.

As a group we critically explored how Honor made diverse connections across teaching, learning, and research. In particular, Honor was enthusiastic about learning more about the reading process through her own inquiry. This iterative process provided recurring opportunities for questioning, reflecting, and synthesizing insights about EMMA data in the context of guided collaboration. This EMMA study shows how before this experience, Honor's understanding of reading involved the need to read words accurately. Her analysis of the substitution of "dishes" for "clothes" revealed this internalized approach to reading. Thus, collaborative and iterative data analysis illuminated both the presence of this approach as well as its inherent contradiction to the theoretical premises foregrounding EMMA research. Honor began to raise questions about her existing paradigm of reading, recognizing the need to attend to readers' comprehending processes during observable acts of reading (Y. Goodman et al., 2005).

Honor found the dialogic nature of the team particularly helpful as she worked through difficult questions about the sociopsycholingusitic model of reading (K. Goodman, 2008). Furthermore, these dialogic exchanges fostered Honor's reflexivity about how the sociopsycholingusitic model of reading (K. Goodman, 2008) informed her own ideas about the nature of reading as well as conducting research in the field. Her process of comprehending supports the idea that the text and the reader are impossible to separate as meaning is co-constructed (Rosenblatt, 2019). The exploration into her own process of comprehending adds nuance to her understanding of the transactional reading model as she made sense of the EMMA data and sociopsycholinguistic knowledge.

Honor, perhaps like other secondary English language arts (ELA) teachers, was unfamiliar with the terminology and concept of language cueing systems. It is not surprising that we would have extended conversations around the value of miscues when the secondary ELA field as a whole has not engaged in such work. Even as secondary English language arts pedagogy has moved to incorporating more reading instruction, there is little take up of the notion of miscue analysis as a potential resource for unpacking adolescent readers' processes. Honor's experiences point to the value in broadening secondary ELA teachers' knowledge base to include holistic approaches to literacy development across the lifespan. Indeed, based upon our experiences presenting our work at professional conferences, we have found secondary ELA teachers eager for information about EMMA and miscue analysis in general. Through the implementation of miscue analysis, she learned more about the usefulness of applied sociopsycholinguistics as a framework.

Our collaborative approach to EMMA research immersed Honor as an emerging researcher in the analysis and reflection of data. Given the amount of knowledge needed to gather EMMA data, as well as the complexities of data analysis as informed by the sociopsycholinguistic transactional reading model, this mentoring and collaboration was a crucial support as she shifted from the paradigm of teacher to researcher. Honor noted, "the nature of this collaboration creates an environment in which I can seek support and feedback as I oscillate between the typical feelings of uncertainty and certainty in doctoral students." We take this as a charge to mentors to continue offering self-study in a collaborative, dialogic context because inherent in the process is a deep examination of the tacit beliefs that underlie teacher-researchers' knowledge and reflexivity.

References

Baye, A., Inns, A., Lake, C., & Slavin, R. E. (2018). A synthesis of quantitative research on reading programs for secondary students. *Reading Research Quarterly, 54*(2), 133–166. doi:10.1002/rrq.229

Beers, K. (2004). *When kids can't read: What teachers can do.* Portsmouth, NH: Heinemann.

Fries, P. H. (2008). Words, context, and meaning in reading. In A. Flurkey, E. Paulson, & K. Goodman (Eds.), *Scientific realism in studies of reading* (pp. 53–82). New York: Lawrence Erlbaum.

Goodman, K. (2008). Miscue analysis as scientific realism. In A. Flurkey, E. Paulson, & K. Goodman (Eds.), *Scientific realism in studies of reading* (pp. 7–21). New York: Lawrence Erlbaum.

Goodman, K., Fries, P. H., & Strauss, S. L. (2016). *Reading: The grand illusion.* New York: Routledge.

Goodman, Y., Watson, D., & Burke, C. (2005). *Reading miscue inventory: From evaluation to instruction* (2nd ed.). Katonah, NY: Richard C. Owen.

McInnes, J. (1962). *The man who kept house.* New York: Abelard-Schumann.

Paulson, E. (2002). Are oral reading word omissions and substitutions caused by careless eye movements? *Reading Psychology, 23*(1), 45–46. https://doi.org/10.1080/0270271023 17345402

Paulson, E., Flurkey, A., Goodman, Y., & Goodman, K. (2003). Eye movements and miscue analysis: Reading from a constructivist perspective. *The Fifty–Second Yearbook of the National Reading Conference, 52*, 343–355.

Porter, H. D., Kim, K., Franzak, J., & MacDonald, K. (2020). Reframing and repositioning college readers' assumptions about reading through Eye Movement Miscue Analysis. *Journal of Adolescent & Adult Literacy, 63*(5), 519–528.

Reynolds, D. (2020). Of research reviews and practice guides: Translating rapidly growing research on adolescent literacy into updated practice recommendations. *Reading Research Quarterly 53*(6), 401-414. Advance online publication. https://doi.org/10.1002/rrq.314

Rosenblatt, L. (2019). The transactional theory of reading and writing. In D. Alvermann, N. Unrau, M. Sailors, & R. Ruddall (Eds.), *Theoretical models and processes of reading* (7th ed., pp. 451–477). New York: Routledge.

SR Research (2017). *EyeLink 1000 Plus User Manual*. Version 1.0.9. Ontario, Canada.

Part IV

Multimodal: Print and Image

7

Using Eye Movements to Understand Relationships Between Images and Meaning Construction

by Poonam Arya and Karen M. Feathers

The National Council of Teachers of English encourages educators to provide opportunities for students to interact with multimodal texts that is, texts that integrate verbal (words) and non-verbal (visual) elements (e.g., Jewitt, 2005; Lemke, 2002; Schwarz, 2006) to prepare effective readers for the 21st century. While the impact of visual elements, such as images, on comprehension has been previously examined, we still have much to learn about how readers make use of visual information throughout the reading process. Some researchers have suggested that images can negatively affect comprehension, especially when images and written text are not congruent (Beck, 1984; Elster & Simons, 1985). Others suggest that images enhance comprehension and memory because information is presented twice (in images and words) (Gyselinck & Tardieu, 1999). Additionally, studies of the impact of images on comprehension have reported increased comprehension in texts containing images, with highest recall of information displayed in the images (Brookshire, Scharff, & Moses, 2002; Purnell & Solman, 1991). Although these studies suggest a relationship between images and comprehension, they do not provide specific information about reader's attention patterns related to images and how those might impact their understanding of text.

In order to gain a deeper understanding of the role that images play as readers construct meaning, we study readers' eye movements. There is consensus that eye movements are manifestations of the reading process in action and "provide[s] the researcher with an excellent nonintrusive methodology that has proved to be a powerful way of studying the workings of the human mind" (Radach & Kennedy, 2004, p. 4). Specifically, eye movements provide valuable information about what readers attend to, in what order, and for how long, making it an ideal method to examine the different ways in which readers interact with verbal and visual information when reading a multimodal text (Gog & Scheiter, 2010). Thus, this chapter examines the relationship between children's use of images as shown by their eye movements during the oral reading of a picture book and their comprehension of the story through retellings.

Conceptual and Empirical Framework

This study is based on a view of reading as a decision-making process centered on the construction of meaning. Based on this view, readers use a variety of processing strategies and story information to comprehend, and they monitor their understanding and take deliberate action when meaning is not maintained (Clay, 1991; Goodman, 2005; Goodman, Fries, & Strauss, 2016; Goodman, K. & Goodman, Y., 2014). Studies using oral reading analysis have provided useful insights about reading processes. However, they do not address the use of non-verbal features such as graphical displays, images, and arrangement on the page (Ainsworth, 2006; Macken-Horiak, 2004; Unsworth, 2006), features that even young children use to construct meaning (Sipe, 2008; Yaden, Smolken & Conlon, 1989). Thus, in this study we examine children's eye movements to focus on the relationship between images and their construction of meaning.

Images and Texts

Images are an integral part of picture books and serve many functions. Fang (1996) lists seven functions of images, including establishing setting, determining mood, defining and developing characters, contributing to textual coherence, and reinforcing verbal text. Kirk (2000) further states that images not only help interpret characters but also extend themes and meanings present in the verbal text. Expanding on this idea, Genette (1997) and Higonnet (1990) suggest that images and words work together to create an aesthetic whole. Sipe (1998) argues that together words and pictures produce an effect that is greater than the sum of the parts, what Sipe calls "synergy." Echoing this view, Moss (1990) refers to this as "interweaving of text and pictures," and Lunn (2003) refers to it as a "marriage of pictures and story."

Further, Nodelman (1988) and Nikolajeva and Scott (2006) suggest that the visual and verbal limit each other, that is, what is read in the verbal text limits what readers might attend to or expect in the visual text, and what is seen in the visual text limits what is given weight in the verbal text. Given this relationship between images and words in which one affects the other, Sipe argues that the reader must fluctuate between the verbal text and the visual text (1998). This suggests that normal reading involves movement between images and words as readers use both to construct meaning. Thus, documenting this movement is important in order to understand children's reading of picture books, as is done in this study.

In addition to the relationship between images and written text, images have their own meaningful order, which portrays the "syntax of story" (Weisner, as cited in Bandré & Button, 2011, p. 54). If this is true, then deletion of images might impact comprehension. Thus, we observe children reading two naturally occurring versions of the same story that differed only in the number of images included and the placement of those images with written text on individual pages.

Eye Movements, Images, and Texts

Eye tracking research in the last twenty years that has examined processing of longer, connected texts has provided evidence about real-time comprehension processes of readers (e.g., Freeman, 2001; Nelson, Damico, & Smith, 2008; Paulson, 2005; Rayner, 2009). However, the focus has been on the reading of verbal text. A few studies have examined children's use of both verbal and visual texts when a storybook is read aloud to them (Evans, Saint-Aubin, & Landry, 2009; Justice, Skibbe, Canning, & Lankford, 2005; Roy-Charland, Saint-Aubin, & Evans, 2007; Verhallen & Bus, 2011). But they do not examine attentional patterns when children read a text themselves. Additionally, these studies present a partial understanding about children's cognitive processing as they only focus on eye movements.

Just and Carpenter (1984) assert that it is useful to combine eye movement data with another measure that looks at what the reader is doing in addition to moving the eyes. Paulson and Henry (2002) recommend complementing eye-movement data with retelling procedures, and Hyönä (2010) suggests, "performance measures, such as retrospective comprehension tests or think-alouds" (p. 173).

Of the few studies that use eye movements and a comprehension measure, Duckett (2002), notes that first graders use both visual and verbal texts, and that saccades between words and images are often caused by difficulties with text processing. Other research with second graders notes that readers' use of images is deliberate, and that they construct meaning from both words and images separately and interactively to strengthen their comprehension (Arya & Feathers, 2012; Liwanag, Pelatti, R. Martens, & P. Martens, 2016). However, none of these studies explore students reading different versions of the same story.

This study uses information provided by both eye movements and retellings as children read two versions of a picture book. Specifically, it examines

the following question: What is the relationship between children's use of images as shown by their eye movements and their comprehension of the story?

Our Study

Participants were 12 third grade children (seven boys and five girls). They attended an after-school university literacy program for 90 minutes per week for
16 weeks. Teachers used fiction and non-fiction trade books, magazines, and
texts created by children for the tutoring. The children who attended the program came from the large urban community in which the university is located
and attended the local schools where language arts instruction was imparted
using the Open Court Reading (SRA/McGraw-Hill, 2002) program. The children varied across ethnicity and socio-economic status, with eight being Black
and four White. Based on the *Qualitative Reading Inventory-5* (*QRI-5*) (Leslie
& Caldwell, 2011), children were reading one year below grade level.

What We Did

Children read two versions of a 370-word second grade story, *The Wolf's Chicken
Stew* (Kasza, 1987) (*Chicken Stew*)—the original story and an adaptation in a
second-grade anthology. There were no variations in the verbal text across the
two versions of the story, but they differed in the number of images and the
arrangement of print and images on two facing pages. The original version of
the story included nine double page spreads and 10 single page images (total
28 images) while the adaptation contained three double page spreads, three
single page images, and one page with three separate images (total 12 images).
The average number of sentences per page for the original and adapted versions
were 1.7 and 3.4 respectively. This story was unfamiliar to children and was a
good match for them based on their reading level as measured by scores on the
QRI-5.

We worked one-on-one with each child in a 30–40 minute session.
Children were randomly assigned to either the original or adapted book version group, with six children in each group. The stories were presented on a
computer that displayed two facing pages of the story in each screen shot; so,
the screen view was the same as if children were looking at the book. Children
controlled movement from one screenshot to another and could take as much
time as they wanted on each screen. While children read, eye movements were
tracked using an Applied Science Laboratories Model 504-Eye Tracker and
Gaze Tracker.

After orally reading the story, children retold the story in their own words.
First, in an unaided retelling, children shared what they remembered and then

we asked open-ended questions (an aided retelling). The oral reading, retelling, and eye fixations were digitally recorded.

To analyze the data, we calculated the total number of fixations and the fixation durations on the words and images. We also examined children's transitions from image to image, text to image or vice versa, in addition to studying their image fixations to determine exactly what children focused on in each image. We analyzed each retelling for evidence of character development, plot events, theme, and inferences/connections and scored out of 100 points (Goodman, Watson & Burke, 2005). We also analyzed the relationship between retelling, the text, and images in the story. To do this, we identified idea units (IUs) in each retelling that were directly related (1) only to images in the story, (2) to both images and the verbal text, (3) to information only in the verbal text, or (4) to inferences made by the reader that are not stated in the text or explicit in the image. We coded and analyzed all the data independently and resolved any disagreements by discussion and revisiting the data.

What We Found

Eye Movement Patterns and Images

Given that the adapted version contained a reduced number of images, there were fewer fixations on images in that version as well as fewer transitions to images (see Table 7.1). These numbers, however, do not provide a complete picture of the fixations and transitions as the distribution across the images varied between the two groups. For example, both groups had the same number of fixations (36) on Image 2A that shows the wolf looking at the chicken from behind a tree in the forest, but children reading the adapted version had

Version of Story	Eye Movement Data				Retelling Data		
	Total # Fixations on Images	Average Fixations per Image	Total # Transitions	Average Transitions per Image	Story Events Recalled	Inferences Made	Total Recall
Original	1335	47.68	389	13.89	58.7%	76.7%	64.4%
Adapted	747	62.25	255	21.25	55.8%	55.0%	56.7%

Table 7.1: Eye Movement and Retelling Data Across Two Versions of *The Wolf's Chicken Stew*
Source: Authors.

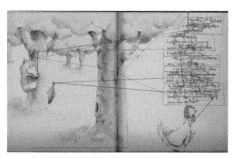

Figure 7.1: Fixations on and Transitions to Images 2A and 2B in Adapted Version (Left) and Original Version (Right) of *The Wolf's Chicken Stew.*

Source: Authors.
Source: All images are from *The Wolf's Chicken Stew* by Keiko Kasza, copyright © 1987 by Keiko Kasza. Used by permission of G. P. Putnam's Sons Books for Young Readers, an imprint of Penguin Young Readers Group, a division of Penguin Random House LLC. All rights reserved.

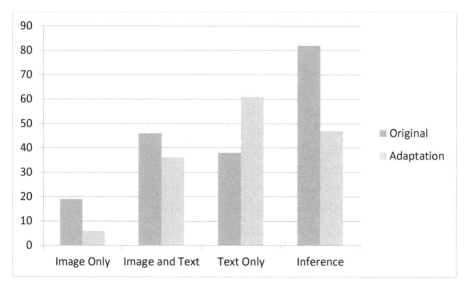

Figure 7.2: Percentage of Retelling Idea Units by Categories for the Two Versions of *The Wolf's Chicken Stew*

Source: Authors.

19 transitions to the image as compared to 9 transitions for those reading the original version (see Figure 7.1). This is probably related to the rearrangement of text in the adaptation which resulted in almost twice the amount of text (7 sentences) accompanying this illustration as opposed to the original version (4 sentences). In other instances, children reading the adaptation had many more fixations on some images. For instance, they had higher number of fixations

(81 vs. 56) and double the number of transitions (25 vs.12) on an image (16B) showing the wolf surrounded by chicks. Further, most of the fixations were on the chicks. Since all the children read the text accompanying this image without miscues, the fixations and transitions were not related to text difficulty. The differences might be because in the adaptation, the chicks are depicted for the first time in this image, but have been pictured in previous images in the original version.

Relationship Between Images and Comprehension
The retelling scores for the children reading the original version ranged from 27%–81%, with an average score of 64.4% and for those reading the adapted version ranged from 26%–74% with an average of 56.7% (Figure 7.2).The differences in overall retelling scores were not big for the children reading the two versions of *Chicken Stew.* However, there were larger differences in the categories that required inferences (plot/theme and subtleties), with the children reading the original version scoring higher (76.7% vs. 55.0%). For example, both Taja (read original story) and Freddy (read adaptation) had similar scores for story events, but Taja scored considerably higher (26.7%) than Freddy (13.3%) on inferences and connections to the story. Taja, who had multiple fixations on the wolf, chicken, and the trees in Images 2A and 2B (Figure 7.1), recalled that "the chicken was walking through the woods" and then continued with an inference that "the chicken didn't know that the wolf was walking behind him." When asked what made her think that, Taja responded by saying, "Because otherwise the chicken would have run away or screamed and run away." Another student Daran, who read the original version of *Chicken Stew*, also made multiple inferences including that after getting a hundred kisses from the chicks, "the wolf felt good [and] that's why Wolf said next time he would bring them [chicks] a hundred cookies."

These differences in the children's retellings led to consideration of the relationship between comprehension and the visual and verbal information in the story. Figure 7.2 shows the percentage of IUs for each version of the story across the categories of image only, image and text, text only, and inferences.

Most of the IUs for children who read the adaptation were connected to text only (41%), whereas this was almost half for those who read the original version (21%). This is expected because there were fewer images in the adaptation and more of the story content had to be gleaned from only the verbal text.

Conversely, children who read the original version of *Chicken Stew* had a higher percentage of IUs that contained information present only in the images (10% vs. 4%). For example, children who read the original version that contained Images 14A and 14B (Figure 7.3) had higher recall of the related content

than those who read the adaptation without those images. Five of the six children who read the original text indicate that the chicken was not fat. Dave said,
"The next day he went to the house and he saw the chicken . . . and he was so
mad that he didn't get it [chicken stew]. Chicken was not fat." Similarly, Daran
recalled, "Then last night he [wolf] thought chicken would be fat . . . then she
[chicken] opened the door and she was small." Taja stated that the "chicken
opened the door, but she was not fat." The ideas about the chicken opening the
door and chicken not being fat or being too small, that Dave, Daran, and Taja
include in their retellings, came unmistakably from their fixations on Images
14A and 14B (Figure 7.3) that show a surprised wolf looking at a thin chicken
standing at the door. In contrast, only two children reading the adapted version
indicate that the chicken opened the door and none of them mentions that the
chicken was not fat. These examples clearly illustrate the negative impact that
missing images have on children's understanding of the story.

Reader inferences were another area that was greatly impacted by images.
Inferences accounted for 44% of the IUs of children who read the original version as opposed to 31% IUs of children who read the adapted version. Further,
inferences generated by the children who read the adaptation only presented a
rationale for the actions of a character (e.g., wolf) as is evident in the following:

> Tony: Then, Wolf found a momma chicken and he was trying to full her up because
> he wanted her nice and fat so he could eat her.

> Cory: Wolf was trying to make the chicken fat so the chicken could be good for his
> stew.

On the other hand, inferences generated by children who read the original
version included in-depth explanations and evaluations of character actions,
personal connections, and comparisons of character's thoughts or expectations
with actual events.

> Dave: The pancakes and the doughnuts are like junk food stuff. I like them too. So,
> if Wolf gives chicken a whole bunch of stuff, then he'll be fat.

> Sierra: The wolf couldn't do nothing. He wasn't as smart enough as the chicken.

> Researcher: Why do you say that?

> Sierra: Because the chicken, he knew what Wolf was trying to do. Chicken is not fat.
> Chicken didn't eat all the food, so the wolf did it for no reason. Wolf didn't get what
> he wanted.

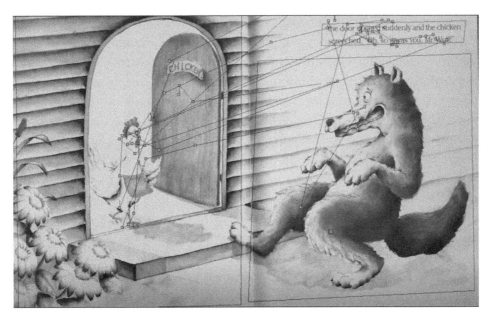

Figure 7.3: Daran's Fixations on and Transitions to Images 14A and 14B in Original Version of *The Wolf's Chicken Stew*

Source: Authors.
Source: All images are from *The Wolf's Chicken Stew* by Keiko Kasza, copyright © 1987 by Keiko Kasza. Used by permission of G. P. Putnam's Sons Books for Young Readers, an imprint of Penguin Young Readers Group, a division of Penguin Random House LLC. All rights reserved.

Many inferences and connections, including the ones above, made by children reading the original text were supported by information present only in the images, highlighting the important relationship between images and comprehension.

Discussion

Using eye movements, in this study we provide information about the relationship between images in stories and readers' comprehension, thus supporting previous research (e.g., Arya & Feathers, 2012; Brookshire et al., 2002; Feathers & Arya, 2015; Purnell & Solman, 1991). Additionally, observations of children's patterns of eye movements show that their eye movements are not random but deliberate (Arya & Feathers, 2012; Just & Carpenter, 1984). Children make use of the image/text relationship to understand the "whole" of the story that is greater than the sum of its parts (Nodelman, 1988; Sipe, 1998).

The important relationship between images and understanding is especially illustrated by the differences in eye movement patterns of children reading the original story versus the adaptation, which contained missing images and altered arrangement of images and text on a page. Children reading the adaptation repeatedly transitioned to images they had on the page for mainly two reasons: (1) the images and text arrangement on a page were altered (e.g., Image 2A). Having additional text on the page that was not supported by the image confused the children as they looked for visual support where there was none; (2) information was presented for the first time in the images (e.g., Image 16B) because previous representations of it were deleted in the adapted version. The rearrangement and missing images disrupted the "syntax" of the story (Weisner as cited in Bandré & Button, 2011), thus affecting not only eye movements but also children's comprehension of the story (Arya & Feathers, 2012; Feathers & Arya, 2015). This also coheres with McCrudden, Schraw, and Hartley (2004), who state that a "poorly organized text imposes greater extraneous cognitive load" (p. 291), making it difficult for readers to integrate ideas in a text.

Further, children who read the original version had different understandings of the story than those who read the adapted version, as shown in their more elaborated retellings and differences in inferences about events and characters. In keeping with Brookshire et al. (2002), children used images to understand the setting as well as characters and their feelings. For example, children reading the original story used the information in Images 14A and 14B to infer that the wolf was mad or surprised that the chicken was not fat (character feelings). Additionally, the information retold by the children was available only in the images. This data is consistent with studies that suggest that information associated with images is more likely to be recalled than information not related to images (Brookshire et al., 2002; Purnell & Solman, 1991), and with theories that point to critical connections between images and understanding (Genette, 1997; Moss, 1990).

Final Thoughts

The results of this study highlight the importance of images in stories and provide evidence that readers use both visual and verbal information during reading. These results add to previous research on the importance of images in understanding texts as well as eye movement research on children (Arya & Feathers, 2012; Brookshire et al., 2002; Duckett, 2002; Feathers & Arya, 2015; Liwanag et al., 2016). Additionally, these findings support theories that propose a relationship between image and text (Nodelman, 1988; Sipe, 1998); they also support what Kress and van Leeuwen (2006) refer to as multimodality.

Most schools today use commercial reading programs that contain adaptations of original texts with deleted images and rearrangements of both images and verbal text (e.g., Arya & Feathers, 2012; Hoffman, Sailors, & Patterson, 2002). Given the findings of this study that highlight the differences in children's reading and understanding of original and adapted versions, more thought should be given to using original literature for classroom reading instruction to promote improved comprehension as well as visual and textual literacy. Additionally, original stories supply children with reading experiences that are similar to what they will encounter in the real world, thus promoting the development of effective reading processes.

In addition to using original literature, data from this study also suggests that teachers should avoid instructional practices that favor verbal text over visual text or disrupt the relationship between the visual and verbal texts. Sipe (2008), for example, does not advocate that teachers conduct "picture walks" through the book (p. 142), as this disrupts the relationship between the visual and verbal text and contradicts the basic premise of picture books that images and words should be encountered together as they form a coherent whole.

Further research needs to be done to more completely understand how children use images in texts to construct understanding. This study involved one group of children reading two versions of one story. Future research should be conducted with children of differing ages and reading proficiencies engaged with many different types of texts. Additionally, the use of eye movement and retelling data in this study demonstrates that future research could benefit from utilizing this methodology to expand our understanding of the relationship between children's use of images and their comprehension and provide valuable insights into the reading process.

References

Ainsworth, S. (2006). DeFT: A conceptual framework for considering learning with multiple representations. *Learning and Instruction, 16*(3), 183–198.

Arya, P., & Feathers, K. (2012). Reconsidering children's readings: Insights into the reading process. *Reading Psychology, 33*(4), 301–322.

Bandré, P. E., & Button, K. (2011). Picturebook design: Art, words, typography . . . everything matters. *Journal of Children's Literature, 37*(1), 54–59.

Beck, I. (1984). Developing comprehension: The impact of the directed reading lesson. In R. C. Anderson, J. Osborn, & R. J. Tierney (Eds.), *Learning to read in American schools: Basal readers and content texts* (pp. 3–20). Mahwah, NJ: Erlbaum.

Brookshire, J., Scharff, L., & Moses, L. (2002). The influence of illustrations on children's book preferences and comprehension. *Reading Psychology, 23*(4), 323–339.

Clay, M. (1991). *Becoming literate: The construction of inner control.* Portsmouth, NH: Heinemann.

Duckett, P. (2002). New insights: Eye fixations and the reading process. *Talking Points, 13*(2), 16–21.

Elster, C., & Simons, H. (1985). How important are illustrations in children's readers? *The Reading Teacher, 39*(2), 148–152.

Evans, M., Saint-Aubin, J., & Landry, N. (2009). Letter names and alphabet book reading by senior kindergarteners: An eye movement study. *Child Development, 80*(6), 1824–1841.

Fang, Z. (1996). Illustrations, text, and the child reader: What are pictures in children's storybooks for? *Reading Horizons, 37*(2), 130–142.

Feathers, K., & Arya, P. (2015). Exploring young children's use of illustrations in a picture book. *Language and Literacy, 17*(1), 42–62.

Freeman, A. (2001). *The eyes have it: Oral miscue and eye movement analyses of the reading of fourth-grade Spanish/English bilinguals* (Unpublished doctoral dissertation). The University of Arizona. Tucson, Arizona.

Genette, G. (1997). *Paratexts: Thresholds of interpretation* (J. Lewin, Trans.). New York: Cambridge University Press.

Gog, T., & Scheiter, K. (2010). Eye tracking as a tool to study and enhance multimedia learning. *Learning and Instruction, 20*(2), 95–99.

Goodman, K. (2005). Making sense of written language: A lifelong journey. *Journal of Literacy research, 37*(1), 1–24.

Goodman, K., Fries, P., & Strauss, S. (2016) *Reading, the grand illusion: How and why people make sense of print*. New York: Routledge.

Goodman, K., & Goodman, Y. (2014). *Making sense of learners, making sense of written language: The selected works of Kenneth S. Goodman and Yetta M. Goodman*. New York: Routledge.

Goodman, Y., Watson, D., & Burke, C. (2005). *Reading miscue inventory: From evaluation to instruction*. New York: R.C. Owen Publishers.

Gyselinck, V., & Tardieu, H. (1999). The role of illustrations in text comprehension: What, when, for whom, and why? In S. R. Goldman & H. van Oostendorp (Eds.), *The construction of mental representations during reading* (pp. 175–195). Mahwah, NJ: Erlbaum.

Higonnet, M. (1990). The playground of the peritext. *Children's Literature Association Quarterly, 15*(2), 47–49.

Hoffman, J., Sailors, M., & Patterson, E. (2002). Decodable texts for beginning reading instruction: The year 2000 basals. *Journal of Literacy Research, 34*(3), 269–298.

Hyönä, J. (2010). The use of eye movements in the study of multimedia learning. *Learning and Instruction, 20*(2), 172–176.

Jewitt, C. (2005). Multimodality, "reading," and "writing" for the 21st century. *Discourse: Studies in the Cultural Politics of Education, 26*(3), 315–331.

Just, M., & Carpenter, P. (1984). Using eye fixations to study reading comprehension. In D. E. Kieras & M. A. Just (Eds.), *New methods in reading comprehension research* (pp. 151–182). Hillsdale, NJ: Lawrence Erlbaum.

Justice, L., Skibbe, L., Canning, A., & Lankford, C. (2005). Pre-schoolers, print and storybooks: An observations study using eye movement analysis. *Journal of Research in Reading, 28*(3), 229–243.

Kasza, K. (1987). *The wolf's chicken stew*. New York: Putnam & Grosset Group.

Kirk, J. (2000). New dimensions word and image in a selection of picture books written by Martin Waddell. In E. Bearne & V. Watson (Eds.), *Where texts and children meet* (pp. 137–145). New York: Routledge.

Kress, G., & van Leeuwen, T. (2006). *Reading images: The grammar of visual design*. New York: Routledge.

Lemke, J. (2002). Travels in hypermodality. *Visual Communication, 1*(3), 299–325.

Leslie, L., & Caldwell, J. (2011). *Qualitative reading inventory*, 5th Ed. New York: Pearson.

Liwanag, M. P., Pelatti, C., Martens, R., & Martens, P. (2016). Children's eye movements, miscue analysis patterns, and retellings when reading a counterpoint picture book. *Literacy Research: Theory, Method, and Practice, 65*, 1–15.

Lunn, J. (2003). The picture book: A commentary. In A. Hudson & S. A. Cooper (Eds.), *Windows and words: A look at Canadian children's literature in English* (pp. 185–190). Ottawa, Ontario, Canada: University of Ottawa Press.

Macken-Horiak, M. (2004). Interacting with the multimodal text: Reflection on image and verbiage in Art Express. *Visual Communication, 3*(1), 5–26.

McCrudden, M., Schraw, G., & Hartley, K. (2004). The influence of presentation, organization, and example context on text learning. *Journal of Experimental Education, 72*(4), 289–306.

Moss, E. (1990). A certain particularity: An interview with Janet and Allen Ahlberg. *Signal, 61*, 20–26.

Nelson, R., Damico, J., & Smith, S. (2008). Applying eye movement miscue analysis to the reading patterns of children with language impairment. *Clinical Linguistics and Phonetics, 22*(4–5), 293–303.

Nikolajeva, M., & Scott, C. (2006). *How picture books work.* New York: Routledge.

Nodelman, P. (1988). *Words about pictures: The narrative art of children's picture books.* Athens: University of Georgia Press.

Paulson, E. (2005). Viewing eye movements during reading through the lens of chaos theory: How reading is like the weather. *Reading Research Quarterly, 40*(3), 338–358.

Paulson, E., & Henry, J. (2002). Does the Degrees of Reading Power assessment reflect the reading process? An eye-movement examination. *Journal of Adolescent & Adult Literacy, 46*(3), 234–244.

Purnell, K., & Solman, R. (1991). The influence of technical illustrations on students' comprehension in geography. *Reading Research Quarterly, 26*(3), 277–299.

Radach, R., & Kennedy, A. (2004). Theoretical perspectives on eye movements in reading: Past controversies, current issues, and an agenda for future research. *European Journal of Cognitive Psychology, 16*(1–2), 3–26.

Rayner, K. (2009). Eye movements and attention in reading, scene perception, and visual search. *Quarterly Journal of Experimental Psychology, 62*(8), 1457–1506.

Roy-Charland, A., Saint-Aubin, J. & Evans, M. (2007). Eye movements in shared book reading with children from kindergarten to grade 4. *Reading and Writing: An Interdisciplinary Journal, 20,* 909–931.

Schwarz, G. (2006). Expanding literacies through graphic novels. *English Journal, 95*(6), 58–64.

Sipe, L. (1998). How picture books work: A semiotically framed theory of text-picture relationships. *Children's Literature in Education, 29(2),* 97–108.

Sipe, L. (2008) Learning from illustrations in picture books. In N. Frey & D. Fisher (Eds.) *Teaching visual literacy* (pp.131–148). Thousand Oaks, CA: Corwin Press.

SRA/McGraw-Hill. (2002). *Open Court Reading.* DeSoto, TX: SRA/McGraw Hill.

Unsworth, L. (2006). Toward a metalanguage for multiliteracies education: Describing the meaning-making resources of language-image interaction. *English Teaching: Practice and Critique, 5*(1), 55–76.

Verhallen, M., & Bus, A. (2011). Young second language learners' visual attention to illustrations in storybooks. *Journal of Early Childhood Literacy, 11*(4), 480–500.

Yaden, D., Smolkin, L., & Conlon, A. (1989). Preschoolers' questions about pictures, print conventions and story text during reading aloud at home. *Reading Research Quarterly, 24*(2), 188–214.

8

Using Eye Movement Miscue Analysis to Examine a Second Grader's Reading Strategies

by Shannon Tucker and Maria Perpetua Socorro U. Liwanag

Reading helps support the literacy development and long-term "reading success" of young readers and is aided by their families (Baker & Scher, 2002). Research shows that positive family literacy experiences and emotions around reading directly influence a child's positive self-concept, which can further influence reading development (Xia, Gu, & Li, 2019; Yeo, Ong, & Ng, 2014).

In this case study (Stake, 2005), Shannon, a parent-researcher, and Maria Perpetua, a literacy researcher, collaborated to examine the reading development of Shannon's second grade son Spencer. Using eye movement miscue analysis (EMMA) we wanted to discover ways Spencer navigated written and pictorial texts that were new and unfamiliar to him to better understand his growth as a reader. Parent-research is not a new approach (Kabuto, 2008). Kabuto and Martens (2014), for instance, highlight many studies by parent-researchers that explore the potential of this inquiry process in examining language, literacy, and education. In this chapter, as parent and literacy researchers, we share how Spencer was intentional and purposeful in using reading strategies to make sense of print and images in two different multimodal texts. We demonstrate how EMMA is an effective tool to explore the relationship between a child's oral reading miscues, retellings, and eye movement patterns.

Contextualizing Our Work

We discuss in this chapter the value of signs and symbols when readers transact with written and pictorial texts. We use social semiotics (Kress & Van Leeuwen, 1996) and the transactional socio-psycholinguistic reading view (Goodman, 1994) as lenses to focus on the roles that signs and symbols play in communication. Sign systems such as written language or art allow cultures to share meaning between individuals (Albers, 2007). These systems are supported by abstract symbols as in alphabetic and non-alphabetic writing systems and images that support communication (Goodman, Fries, & Strauss, 2016).

Social semiotics provides a framework to consider the modal affordances of signs and symbols, including their design and composition in the socio-cultural context of the reader and their influence on meaning construction by readers (Jewitt & Henriksen, 2016; Kress & Van Leeuwen, 1996). The words and images in the two texts selected for this study are categorized as complementary (Nikolajeva & Scott, 2006)—the words and pictures "fill each other's gaps" (p. 12). In complimentary relationships, the pictorial text only adds descriptions of the characters' actions and appearances to the written text without further enhancing the narrative. The pictorial text cannot stand independently from the written text.

The transactional socio-psycholinguistic view of reading (Goodman, 1994; Goodman et al., 2016) enables us to examine language processes and how readers make sense of language and their world. We explore how texts and readers' sociocultural experiences, background knowledge, and linguistic knowledge support strategies that help them create meaning.

What We Did

Eye Movement Miscue Analysis

Eye Movement Miscue Analysis (EMMA) shows how readers transact with texts during oral readings and their eye movement data reveal readers' cognitive processes as they construct meaning (Paulson & Freeman, 2003). While one's eye movements during reading may seem like a smooth process, they are actually complex, with the eyes making many small rapid eye movements (saccades) and brief pauses (fixations) that form the physiological and cognitive basis of vision (Holmqvist, Nystrom, Andersson, Dewhurst, Jarodzka, & de Weijer, 2011; Paulson & Freeman, 2003).

This case study integrates qualitative data from our observations of Spencer's readings with quantitative miscue and eye movement data to explore how he transacts with texts (Stake, 2005). In EMMA, eye movement and oral reading patterns have the potential to visibly reveal the dynamic strategies readers use (Goodman et al., 2016). Exploring eye movement patterns includes analyzing fixations, fixation location, fixation duration, and relationship of the fixations to the miscues produced by the reader. Examining eye movement data from a social semiotic perspective entails understanding both a reader's socio-cultural experiences and their experiences with a variety of texts to help researchers take a reader's prior experiences into account in the meaning-making process

(Hannus & Hyona, 1999). The text and image relationships in books require greater understanding of how readers navigate the time and spatial sequences present in a multimodal form (Kress & Van Leeuwen, 2001). In a multimodal form, written and pictorial texts offer varying ways of supporting meaning. In the texts we used in this study the written and the complementary pictorial texts encode details of character appearance and action, adding to how the stories are represented.

EMMA data for this study were collected using a Tobii X3-120 eye tracker. Spencer's readings of the two texts were structured over a single afternoon. Each reading was created independently in Tobii Studio Pro to allow a break between reading sessions. Prior to each oral reading, we calibrated the Tobii X3-120 eye tracker to Spencer's eye movements using a 5-point calibration test and provided instructions on how to use the mouse to navigate the text. Spencer was also instructed to read out loud as he would read at home, and if he came to something he did not know, to "do his best" during his reading. After the oral readings, oral unaided and aided retellings immediately followed.

Following the readings and retellings, we analyzed the audio and video recordings using Miscue Analysis Classroom Procedure (Goodman, Watson, & Burke, 2005). Here, we marked Spencer's miscues and examined how his miscues influenced each sentence in the context of the text he read. We analyzed his miscues by asking if the sentence was syntactically and semantically acceptable, the degree of meaning change, and the degree of sound and graphic similarity.

To explore how Spencer used complementary images to support his reading, we related his eye movement data and reading miscues to the multimodal design of the text and spatial relationship between written and pictorial texts on each page (Holsanova, 2014; Liwanag, Pelatti, Martens, & Martens, 2016). Using scanpaths and heatmaps, we examined Spencer's reading strategies between text and images to reinforce story details and character identities.

In scanpath visualizations, fixations are represented by circles superimposed on a visual map of what readers looked at when they read the text (Paulson & Freeman, 2003). Heatmaps typically use warm to cool color gradients to represent areas of many fixations (dark gray) and fewer fixations (light gray) (Holmqvist et al., 2011). Using the scanpath and heatmap data, we can visualize what the reader paid attention to and the amount of time (fixation duration) the reader fixated on particular areas when reading. This reveals the "eye-mind hypothesis" (Just & Carpenter, 1980) of a reader's cognitive processing. By analyzing the eye movements in tandem with miscue analysis, we examined patterns evident in Spencer's individual readings and across both texts.

The Reader

At the time of the study, Spencer was a seven-year-old White male second-grader. He lived in an urban setting within the mid-Atlantic region of the United States with his parents and younger sister in a middle-class household. Like Shannon, Spencer's father was a professional who worked outside the home.

Spencer was described as a highly proficient reader, with a Fountas and Pinnel reading level of Q (at the end of second grade). Spencer's academic reading was varied and included grade-level fiction and nonfiction texts. For leisure reading, Spencer preferred the graphic novel genre, selecting popular book series with familiar characters. At the time of this study, Spencer's most recent readings included *Big Nate* (Pierce, 2010), *The Adventures of Captain Underpants* (Pilkey, 1997), and *Dog Man* (Pilkey, 2016).

Text Selections

The texts Spencer read were stand-alone passages from *Ramona Quimby, Age 8* (Cleary, 2009) (fiction) and *Who Was Amelia Earhart?* (Boehm Jerome, 2002) (nonfiction). These readings were selected based on grade-level appropriateness, interest, text density, and Spencer's unfamiliarity with them. In this study, we also had the benefit of Shannon's insightful parent knowledge of reading materials at home and those borrowed from local public libraries to help ensure the texts would be new and engaging to Spencer.

We selected the fiction book *Ramona Quimby, Age 8* (Cleary, 2009) (*Ramona Quimby*) based on Spencer's interest and the book's high text-to-image ratio. Due to the extended length of the first chapter, a passage containing 473 words and one image (473:1 text-to-image ratio) was selected from the beginning of chapter one. Although short, the passage we selected was cohesive and we believed it would be interesting to Spencer, who would soon to be third grader like Ramona. The selected passage introduced Ramona and her family, including descriptions of the main characters and changes in life for the upcoming school year. During the reading, the text was presented over two pages. An illustration of the Quimby family eating breakfast was presented at the conclusion of the text passage showing all the main characters and their actions at the family breakfast table.

The nonfiction text, *Who Was Amelia Earhart?* by Kate Boehm Jerome (2002) (*Amelia Earhart*), was selected based on the series inclusion in grade-level reading guides and its medium text-to-image ratio. As compared to *Ramona Quimby*, this book included 189 words and three images in the first chapter with a 63:1 text-to-image ratio. We selected this text based on a lack of exposure to the historical figure in Spencer's prior coursework and a past interest in aviation. Presented as three single pages with illustrations on each page, this text introduced Spencer to Earhart's status as an early pioneer in aviation.

The use of texts with two different text-to-image ratios was an intentional choice to help us examine how Spencer adapted his reading strategies across text genres with varied use of author description and multimodal page layouts. Spencer read *Ramona Quimby* first followed by *Amelia Earhart*.

What We Learned

Below we explain what we learned about Spencer's miscues, comprehension, and patterns of eye movement data.

Book Titles	Syntactic Acceptability	Semantic Acceptability	Meaning Change			Word Substitution						Holistic Score	Eye Movement Data			
						Graphic Similarity			Sound Similarity				Fixations on Words		Fixations on Images	
			Yes	No	Partial	High	Some	None	High	Some	None		% of Fixations	Mean Fixation Duration	% of Fixations	Mean Fixation Duration
Ramona Quimby, Age 8	96% (Y)	89% (Y)	0%	92%	8%	92%	8%	0%	92%	0%	8%	2 / 5 (40%)	95%	.42 seconds	5%	.29 seconds
Who was Amelia Earhart	100% (Y)	100% (Y)	0%	100%	0%	100%	0%	0%	100%	0%	0%	4 / 5 (80%)	92%	.26 seconds	8%	.20 seconds

Table 8.1: Spencer's Eye Movement Miscue Analysis Data

Source: Authors

Note: Texts read by Spencer were excerpts from *Ramona Quimby, age 8* (Cleary, 2009, pp. 1–4) and *Who was Amelia Earhart?* (Boehm Jerome, 2002, pp. 1–3).

Oral Readings, Comprehension, and EMMA Data: Ramona Quimby, Age 8

Table 8.1 provides Spencer's miscue analysis scores and eye movement data for his readings of the two texts. Spencer's oral reading of *Ramona Quimby, Age 8* (Cleary, 2009) shows his strong knowledge of language and its use. His 96% syntactic acceptability score demonstrates his awareness of how language works and that he uses his knowledge of language patterns in comprehending sentences. His 89% semantic acceptability score shows that he is aware of the story structure and often predicts the text meaning. His miscues did not change the meaning of the sentence in the context of the story 92% of the time. Spencer's substitutions also showed a high graphic and sound similarity of 92%, respectively.

Despite Spencer's high scores with his comprehending process, his holistic comprehension score of 40% for this text suggests that despite a high percentage of syntactic and semantic acceptability, he still did not fully comprehend the passage from *Ramona Quimby* that he read. For this text, we intentionally selected passages from the beginning of Chapter 1 to ensure Spencer did not need additional background information while reading. This limited the amount of character action in the story. While we believe that lack of character action could have contributed to Spencer's limited understanding of the story, we also feel that the use of unfamiliar vocabulary/concepts and his miscues of a key character's name led to confusion on succeeding details about story context, as we discuss below. This then led to misconception regarding the plot and character identities.

Some key features of his reading of the passage from *Ramona Quimby* that we believe impacted his comprehension include character names and description. For example, in the introduction of Ramona's sister "Beatrice," Spencer substituted "Beat-Rice" for "Beatrice" (Figure 8.1). He left this uncorrected and also miscued on Beatrice's nickname "Beezus" by substituting "Beets."

Beat-rice
to her big sister, Beatrice, at breakfast.

Figure 8.1: *Ramona Quimby, Age 8:* Uncorrected Miscue "Beatrice"
Source: Cleary, B. (2009, p. 1). *Ramona Quimby, age 8*. New York: HarperCollins.

We suspect that Spencer's difficulty with the character's name and his unfamiliarity with a strategy for handling names flustered him and influenced his comprehension. He missed key details regarding the characters and relationship dynamics between the sisters. While Spencer was able to describe details about Mr. Quimby's occupation, he could not identify Ramona and Beatrice and fully explain their age relationship. After the EMMA session ended, Spencer discussed the day with Shannon and mentioned he "never heard" the name Beatrice before.

While oral reading miscues provide insight on syntactic and semantic knowledge on meaning construction, the addition of eye movement data in EMMA allows a comprehensive analysis of the text as a whole during an oral reading. In Spencer's miscue substitution of "Beat-Rice" for Beatrice, his attention to this miscue was evident in the dark gray intensity of the heatmap, which also represents multiple fixations on the phrase "Beatrice, at breakfast" (see Figure 8.1).

In addition to terminology confusion, during his reading of the *Ramona Quimby* text, Spencer visibly lost his place briefly as indicated by eye movement data, requiring him to rescan the page to find his lost place before resuming the oral reading. To contextualize these findings holistically, we discussed

Spencer's reading history in depth to better understand his reading interests. In our review of Spencer's recent leisure reading history, we thought his focus on action oriented graphic novels perhaps explained his observed disinterest in the heavy expository text. We don't know, however, if/how his reading of an action-oriented text with similar text density might have been different.

Oral Readings, Comprehension, and EMMA data: Who Was Amelia Earhart?
In comparison, Spencer's syntactic and semantic acceptability scores were 100% for his reading of *Amelia Earhart*. Spencer produced six miscues that were all 100% in graphic and sound similarly. His 80% comprehension score shows his understanding of the text when he gave details about Amelia Earhart and supported facts he remembered in his retelling. A miscue example in Figure 8.2 is the nonword "$pirit" which Spencer immediately corrected when he looked again, indicated by the intensity of the heat map and demonstrating his reading strategies.

she had a special spirit She liked to be the first to do new things.

Figure 8.2: *Who Was Amelia Earhart?*: Corrected Nonword Miscue for "$pirit"
Source: Boehm Jerome, K. (2002, p. 1). *Who was Amelia Earhart?* New York: Penguin Putnam Books for Young Readers.

Where the *Ramona Quimby* passage included multiple characters and rich character detail, the biographical focus of *Amelia Earhart* provided a focused fact-based narrative rather than development of character dynamics and motivation. This coupled with Spencer's interest in aviation and the direct use of images to support and extend main ideas helped support his understanding of story content.

Reading Strategy: Multimodal Reading Strategies of Text and Images
The varied use of print and complementary images across texts provides an opportunity to view how Spencer transacted with written text and images to construct meaning in context. In his transaction with the written texts, his eye movement data record (see Table 8.1) shows that 95% of his fixations were on the written text when reading *Ramona Quimby*. We believe that the high text-to-image ratio of this passage contributed to the high percentage of fixations. Since the passage was also the beginning of the chapter in this narrative text, the author was still building the content and characters, so Spencer carefully focused his attention on the written text to familiarize himself with the story.

In reading *Amelia Earhart*, 92% of Spencer's fixations were on the written text. He also gathered information about this nonfiction text and paid careful attention to the description of Amelia Earhart. The percentages of Spencer's fixations for both texts were similar (95% vs. 92%) despite the length of the texts and the number of images, indicating his focus on making meaning in the written text.

Spencer's mean fixation duration of .42 seconds for *Ramona Quimby* compared to .26 seconds for *Amelia Earhart* perhaps shows how the lack of character action in *Ramona Quimby* and being unfamiliar with some names influenced his mean fixation duration and indicates how hard he was working to make sense of his reading. Spencer's syntactic and semantic acceptability scores of 100% in *Amelia Earhart* show his familiarity with the language and concepts of this passage and thus his shorter mean fixations duration. EMMA studies (Duckett, 2002; Goodman et al., 2016) confirm that readers focus longer on unfamiliar concepts than familiar ones.

We also see Spencer's consistent use of images to support the main ideas and aid in passage comprehension across texts. Spencer used images to reinforce character identities and facts using images during and following his reading of text passages. In the Ramona Quimby text, Spencer shifted reading strategies from the first to the second page with the introduction of an illustration of the Quimby family at breakfast. Where the initial text passages on page one focused on Ramona and her sister Beezus, page two focused on the occupations and descriptions of Ramona's parents Mr. and Mrs. Quimby. Initially when viewing page two, Spencer briefly glanced at the image of the Quimby

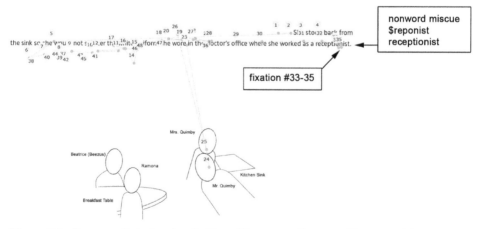

Figure 8.3: *Ramona Quimby, Age 8: Use of Images to Support Character Identity.*

Source: Cleary, B. (2009, p. 2). *Ramona Quimby, age 8*. New York: HarperCollins.

family. During his reading, Spencer paused when characters were referenced. As an example (see Figure 8.3), when reading about Mrs. Quimby's uniform and occupation as a "receptionist," Spencer paused and briefly glanced at the mother's (fixation #25) and father's (fixation # 24) faces before resuming his reading.

In *Who Was Amelia Earhart?* the text on the first page reads, "*Amelia Earhart was a pioneer . . . She liked to be the first to do new things.*" The image shows a character in a pilot suit standing in front of a plane. Spencer focused on the character's face following his reading of the passage (see also Figure 8.3). This pattern of image use is found in subsequent passages, when encountering "her" or "airplane" as well. Spencer would pause and then look at Amelia's face or the propellers on the airplane, the meaning of these passages through thematic repetition; that is, the images add meaning that the words provide (Krashen, 2004). In much the same way as when students read multiple texts to engage deeply on a topic, the passages and images here also provided that opportunity for Spencer to consolidate knowledge of what he was reading to make sense. We believe that Spencer's use of images helped support his understanding of the character and topic just as authors Liwanag and Dresbach (2012) found in their study about multimodal texts using EMMA where preservice teachers looked at the faces of individuals while viewing the multimedia of their peers' self-designed book trailers of young adult literature to better understand the character's emotions and story content.

Where the image of Amelia Earhart reinforces Earhart's identity and her role as a pilot, the complexity of the text and limited use of images in *Ramona Quimby* provides minimal support to clarify Spencer's understanding of the relationship between the sisters by only depicting the action of the Quimby breakfast table. This limits his ability to self-correct and make meaning from the text. Although we selected a complete passage for this particular reading, we believe that allowing Spencer to read further would help clarify some of the content/vocabulary in *Ramona Quimby* by providing more character context and the inclusion of additional supporting illustrations.

When comparing his fixations on the images in both texts, we see a slight difference in percentage and mean fixation duration. His 5% fixations on the *Ramona Quimby* images and 8% fixations on *Amelia Earhart* images may be attributed to the nature of the image as "filling the gap" of the text but not really adding anything to enhance the story. The mean fixation duration for the images shows how Spencer occasionally utilized the images to support his reading.

Discussion

Our case study of Spencer's reading show similarities and differences in how he read the two different multimodal texts. Despite differences in length and text-to-image ratios, Spencer's syntactic and semantic acceptability scores and graphic and sound similarity scores for the two passages were similar as were the number of fixations on written texts versus images (see Table 8.1). His strategy in both texts was to focus primarily on the written text and fixate on the faces of characters in the images to make meaning. Even with these similarities, however, Spencer's retelling scores and fixation durations were quite different. Though his readings "sounded" like his understandings must be comparable too, this was not the case. Topic, readers' interest, and unfamiliar concepts, names, etc., affect comprehension (Goodman et al., 2016; Murphy, 2020).

As literacy researchers (one also a parent-researcher), we acknowledge the sociocultural factors that influence our children's experiences with books. This role is important in the analysis of Spencer's reading of the passage from *Ramona Quimby* to understand the factors that may have contributed to his miscues and lack of comprehension even as a highly proficient reader.

In Spencer's reading of *Ramona Quimby*, understanding his daily vocabulary and prior exposure to new terms in both family and school settings is important to contextualize observed miscues. "Beatrice" and associated nickname "Beezus" were unfamiliar names and likely contributed to Spencer's difficulties with them. Also, the terms "primary" and "secondary" were used to describe the school and contextualize the age relationship between Ramona and Beezus, when Spencer is more familiar with the terms "elementary" or "middle" school, presenting a sociocultural disconnect that was important for meaning development.

Across all of Spencer's readings, he made miscues and used varied reading strategies such as self-correcting and rereading passages in an attempt to make sense of his reading. Despite a high percentage of fixation on the text, Spencer did not fixate on every word (see Figures 8.1, 8.2, and 8.3), a finding also supported by previous EMMA research (Duckett, 2002; Goodman et al., 2016). Spencer's readings showed his use of images and text as reading cues provided context and knowledge of what he was reading. His use of text and image in the story demonstrate the value of multimodal texts in supporting young readers' sense-making process.

Parent Involvement

EMMA provides a holistic view of children's reading strategies, vocabulary, and motivation, giving context to children's academic performance. Parent home observations of reading behaviors such as reading frequency, book selection, and genre selection provide meaningful context to researchers around reading motivation and text familiarity. As a parent-researcher, Shannon's involvement in Spencer's day-to-day life provided important insights on the socio-cultural context of his meaning-making. Without parental involvement in research, we would be unable to confirm how vocabulary knowledge and prior experience influenced comprehension.

Parents, teachers, and parent-researchers can help support children by encouraging a variety of reading materials and genres to support literacy and knowledge development in order to value and expand children's socio-cultural experiences. By supporting genre affinity in addition to topic affinity in reading materials, parents can further support a child's self-perception as a reader.

Implications

When selecting texts, we encourage teachers to evaluate text complexity on a variety of dimensions, to apply this to their classrooms and the needs of their readers, and to help parents advocate for their children by understanding how to use information about various reading levels and content to nurture their children's reading growth. Using only reading levels would not provide insight on vocabulary (e.g., unfamiliar names and alternative descriptions such as "primary/secondary school"), structure, and knowledge/concepts needed for a child to make sense of a text. While they can be helpful, reading levels do not address the qualitative dimensions of a text's complexity like structure, language conventionality, and knowledge demands on our children (Short, Lynch-Brown, & Tomlinson, 2018), so understanding how all these factors can influence students engagement in reading is significant.

We show in this study how EMMA is an important tool to help families understand how children transact with various genres of texts. It provides a powerful way to explore children's reading strategies as it relates to their lived experiences. Showing the strategies children use to make meaning from text and images through EMMA, helps support young readers like Spencer in their reading development.

References

Albers, P. (2007). *Finding the artist within: Creating and reading visual texts in the English language classroom.* Newark, DE: International Reading Association.

Baker, L., & Scher, D. (2002). Beginning readers' motivation for reading in relation to parental beliefs and home reading experiences. *Reading Psychology, 23*(4), 239–269.

Boehm Jerome, K. (2002). *Who was Amelia Earhart?* New York: Penguin Putnam Books for Young Readers.

Cleary, B. (2009). *Ramona Quimby, age 8.* New York: HarperCollins.

Duckett, P. (2002). New insights: Eye fixations and the reading process. *Talking Points, 13*(2), 16–21.

Goodman, K. (1994). Reading, writing, and written texts: A transactional sociopsycholinguistic view. In R. B. Ruddell, M. R. Ruddell, & H. Singer (Eds.), *Theoretical models and processes of reading* (4th ed., pp. 1093–1130). Newark, DE: International Reading Association.

Goodman, K., Fries, P. H., & Strauss, S. L. (2016). *Reading, the grand illusion: How and why people make sense of print*. New York: Routledge.

Hannus, M., & Hyönä, J. (1999). Utilization of illustrations during learning of science textbook passages among low-and high-ability children. *Contemporary Educational Psychology, 24*(2), 95–123.

Holmqvist, K., Nyström, M., Andersson, R., Dewhurst, R., Jarodzka, H., & de Weijer, J. (2011). *Eye tracking: A comprehensive guide to methods and measures*. Oxford: Oxford University Press.

Holsanova, J. (2014). Reception of multimodality: Applying eye-tracking methodology in multimodal research. In C. Jewitt (Ed.), *Routledge Handbook of Multimodal Analysis* (2nd ed., pp. 285–296). London: Routledge.

Jewitt, C., & Henriksen, B. (2016). Social Semiotic Multimodality. In N.-M. Klug & H. Stöckl (Eds.), *Handbook Language in Multimodal Context* (pp. 145–164). Berlin, Germany: de Gruyter.

Just, M. A., & Carpenter, P. A. (1980). A theory of reading: From eye fixation to comprehension. *Psychological Review, 87*(4), 329–354.

Kabuto, B. (2008). Parent-research as a process of inquiry: An ethnographic perspective. *Ethnography & Education, 3*(2), 177–194.

Kabuto, B., & Martens, P. (Eds.). (2014). *Linking families, learning, and schooling: Parent–researcher perspectives*. New York: Routledge.

Krashen, S. (2004). The case for narrow reading. *Language Magazine, 3*(5), 17–19.

Kress, G. R., & Van Leeuwen, T. (1996). *Reading images: The grammar of visual design*. New York: Routledge.

Kress, G., & Van Leeuwen, T. (2001). *Multimodal discourse*. New York: Bloomsbury Academic.

Liwanag, M., & Dresbach, S. (2012). Reading multimodally: Designing and developing multimedia literacy projects through an understanding of Eye Movement Miscue Analysis (EMMA). *Journal of Interactive Technology and Pedagogy*, Issue 1, Spring 2012. https://jitp.commons.gc.cuny.edu/reading-multimodally-designing-and-developing-multimedia-literacy-projects-through-an-understanding-of-eye-movement-miscue-analysis-emma/

Liwanag, M. P. S. U., Pelatti, C. Y., Martens, R., & Martens, P. (2016). Children's eye movements, miscue analysis patterns, and retellings when reading a counterpoint picture book. *Literacy Research: Theory, Method, and Practice, 65*(1), 253–267. https://doi.org/10.1177/2381336916661535

Murphy, S. (2020). *Sense-making and shared meaning in language and literacy education*. New York: Routledge.

Nikolajeva, M., & Scott, C. (2006). *How picturebooks work*. New York: Routledge.

Paulson, E. J., & Freeman, A. E. (2003). *Insight from the eyes: The science of effective reading instruction*. Portsmouth, NH: Heinemann.

Pierce, L. (2010). *Big Nate: In a class by himself*. New York: United Feature Syndicate Inc.

Pilkey, D. (1997). *The adventures of Captain Underpants*. New York: Blue Sky Press/Scholastic Inc.

Pilkey, D. (2016). *Dog Man*. New York: Graphix/Scholastic Inc.

Short, K., Lynch-Brown, C., & Tomlinson, C. (2018). *Essentials of children's literature*. New York: Pearson.

Stake, R. E. (1995). *The art of case study research*. Thousand Oaks, CA: Sage Publications Inc.

Xia, T., Gu, H., & Li, W. (2019). Effect of parents' encouragement on reading motivation: The mediating effect of reading self-concept and the moderating effect of gender. *Frontiers in Psychology, 10*, 609.

Yeo, L. S., Ong, W. W., & Ng, C. M. (2014). The home literacy environment and preschool children's reading skills and interest. *Early Education and Development, 25*(6), 791–814.

9

Reading Print and Visuals in Sixth Grade Science Texts

Insights From EMMA

by Yueh-Nu Hung

Reading is an important tool for learning in science. Hines, Wible, and McCartney (2010) wrote that ". . . good literacy skills make it easier to learn science, but science topics can also be used to teach literacy skills that will translate well to other subjects" (p. 447). Authentic hands-on activities and observation are important in science class, but some scientific concepts cannot be manipulated or observed. For example, it is difficult to see atoms with school science lab equipment and not possible to manipulate the phases of the moon in the lab. In these cases, students rely on reading to learn and inquire about the scientific concepts.

Multiple representations using multi-modality are defining features of science text. Non-verbal visuals assist in the presentation, interpretation, and elaboration of complex concepts. Helping students to read visuals and integrate information from text and visuals are an important goal in science education and disciplinary literacy (Eilam & Gilbert, 2014).

Eye-tracking technology is often used to understand how people read science texts and visuals. With the addition and juxtaposition of oral reading miscue information, eye movement miscue analysis (EMMA) research provides more in-depth information about the visual and cognitive processes of reading comprehension.

The purposes of this chapter are twofold. First, I show how EMMA research methods allow literacy practitioners and researchers to see readers' various visual and cognitive meaning making processes when reading print and visuals in science text. Second, I report major findings from Hung's (2014) EMMA research using science text and discuss implications on science reading instruction. To begin, though, I first discuss the features and challenges of reading science texts to contextualize what follows.

Science Texts: Features and Challenges

A large number of science texts are informational and are sometimes referred to as nonfiction. Many children develop literacy knowledge from reading stories and fiction, but nonfiction accounts for most of the school tests and most of the reading that adults do in everyday life (Moss, 2005). As young children move up in school grade levels, there is a higher need to rely on reading, especially reading informational text, to complete learning activities in the school. In the United States Common Core State Standards emphasize the importance of reading informational texts, and teachers and schools work hard to provide them, many of which are science related, in the reading curriculum.

Science informational text is usually considered more challenging for young children because of features that are different from stories or narration. In Duke's (2000) study of the scarcity of informational text reading materials and classroom instruction in the early grades in American schools, she defines information text as having many or all of the following features:

> (a) a function to communicate information about the natural or social world, typically from one presumed to be more knowledgeable on the subject to one presumed to be less so; (b) an expectation of durable factual content; (c) timeless verb constructions; (d) generic noun constructions; (e) technical vocabulary; (f) classificatory and definitional material; (g) comparative/contrastive, problem/solution, cause/effect, or like text structures; (h) frequent repetition of the topical theme; and (i) graphical elements such as diagrams, indices, page numbers, and maps. (p. 205)

Discussing the characteristics of science language, Zwiers (2008) says that science language uses many nominalizations and generalized verbs in the present tense and connects abstract ideas with illustrations of various media. Fang (2006) points out that science text is difficult because the language used in science is distinctly remote from everyday life language. The technical vocabulary, ordinary words with meanings that are disciplinary specific, abstract nouns, ellipses, complex sentences, and passive voice are just a few aspects of science text that make reading it challenging for students. Fang (2008) further summarizes four different causes for the difficulty of reading science text: technicality, abstraction, density, and authoritativeness.

One of the main challenges in reading science informational text is understanding the non-verbal images and integrating information from text and visuals. Different types of images serve different purposes in the representation of meaning. Carney and Levin (2002) divide the non-verbal images into four categories based on the different functions they serve. The first type is representational pictures that show what the verbal text states in non-verbal ways by providing the same or parallel information. The second type is organizational pictures that arrange the text information in a visual and structural framework. The third is interpretational pictures that explain what is said in the verbal text and provide more information to clarify the concepts or ideas. The fourth type is transformational or mnemonic pictures that help students to go beyond the visual information and move to higher cognitive application tasks. In an earlier discussion Levin (1981) identifies decorational pictures that are created to enhance the attractiveness of books or texts, but bear little or no relationship to the meaning of the text.

Due to the multiple representational and multimodal nature of science text, science and literacy educators develop instructional strategies to help students pay attention to and use information from images which is necessary for the students' comprehension. However, these questions remain: Do students really look at the images? How are the images read? Traditional reading comprehension assessment tools measure the result of comprehension, not the process of viewing or comprehending. Think-aloud protocols ask readers to say what they think at the moment of reading. However, think-aloud research has limitations, such as the reader's degree of readiness or openness to read and talk at the same time, and the less than authentic task of reading in this way. Eye-tracking technology addresses these questions while avoiding the limitations of alternative methods.

Eye-tracking technology makes it possible for teachers and researchers to "see" what the reader is focusing on at the time of reading (Paulson & Freeman, 2003). With a history of more than one hundred years, eye movement studies have a wide range of applications in research on attention and cognition. In what Rayner (1978, 1998) calls the third era of eye movement research that started from mid-1970s, because of advances in eye movement recording and analysis technology, a large number of eye movement studies emerged to examine the cognitive processes in reading and information processing. Eye movement information reveals the complex socio-cognitive processes of meaning construction in reading (Conklin, Pellicer-Sánchez, & Carrol, 2018; Just & Carpenter, 1984; Paulson and Freeman, 2003; Rayner, Chace, Slattery, & Ashby, 2006). Examining a reader's eye movements together with their oral reading performances and miscues creates a powerful tool to "see" what the reader sees, hear what the reader reads aloud, and understand what the reader might have understood or misunderstood. Chapter 2 of this book presents a short history of eye movement research, reading miscue research, and the integration of the two as a research tool (called EMMA) and its application in reading research. With this background, I now share an EMMA study that involves the reading of science text to show how EMMA helps us to understand the reading of print and pictures.

Grade Six Students Reading About Honeybees: An EMMA Study

I conducted this study (Hung, 2014) specifically to explore the questions of visual attention on the verbal text and the non-verbal images when reading science text. To understand readers' attention to print and images in the text, I collected eye movement and oral reading miscue data. Based on EMMA data, I also probed questions about the possible relationships between viewing patterns and comprehension.

The participants were six grade-six elementary school students in Taiwan, where grade six is the last year in the elementary school. The students read a double-page spread of a science text that describes how honeybees dance to tell other bees where to find the food source. The text was written in traditional Chinese characters and had various types of print and images.

This science text, titled *How Do Bees Communicate?* (蜜蜂如何傳達訊息), explains that honeybees dance to tell other bees where honey and pollen are. It also describes how bees use the sun as a reference to locate food sources.

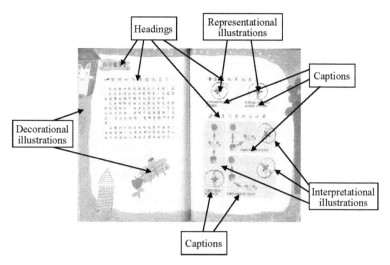

Figure 9.1: Science Text (*Ke xue tong hua 1* [*Science story book series 1*] by C.-G. Hung, 2005)

Sources: Hung, Y.-N. (2014). What are you looking at? An eye movement exploration in science text reading. *International Journal of Science and Mathematics Education, 12*(2), 247.
Original Text: Hung, C.-G. (2005, p. 72). *Ke xue tong hua 1* [*Science story book series 1*]. Taipei: Parenting Source Press, Inc.

There are three different types of print in this science text: headings, main text, and captions. There are also three different types of illustrations: decorational, representational, and interpretational. Figure 9.1 shows the science text and the various print and image sections of it. There are four headings, two paragraphs of main text, and five captions that accompany illustrations. The decorational illustrations are there to beautify the text with little or no reference to the contents of the text. The representational illustrations show messages that are parallel to the contents of the text. The interpretational illustrations augment the text and present information that would be otherwise difficult to say in verbal language.

Data Gathering and Analysis

For this study I used an EyeLink 1000 eye tracker to collect readers' eye movements. This eye tracker does not require the reader to wear or put on any gear on the head, mouth, or body when reading, which makes the reading event closer to real life and less like a lab experiment. For the reading of the written text, I used Goodman, Watson, and Burke's (2005) classroom procedure to collect and analyze miscue data.

The double-page spread of the text was displayed on the computer screen. I instructed the sixth graders to read the text aloud and try to understand the meaning, taking as much time as they needed. Upon finishing the read aloud, I first asked the students to retell what they understood and remembered from the text (unaided retelling). After that, I asked questions to further check their comprehension (aided retelling). I used a retelling guide that I created to evaluate the readers' understandings of specific information, general information, and major concepts.

The first type of eye movement measure I used to answer research questions is the total number of fixations in each print and image area in relation to the size of the area. This is done by dividing the number of fixations in an area by the number of pixels in that area. This information tells me how densely an area is fixated. Next, mean fixation duration in each area is calculated. A longer fixation duration usually suggests a higher degree of attention and more active cognitive processing (Conklin et al., 2018; Rayner et al., 2006; Samuels, Rasinski, & Hiebert, 2011). Mean saccade size in each area is also calculated. When the text is more difficult, the saccade size is usually smaller (Rayner et al., 2006). The saccade size is indicated in Chinese character spaces. Last, I created a heat map, which is a visual presentation of the amount of the fixation time spent on different parts of the text. Areas that receive more fixation time or attention will be more red or hot in this color-coded display. I also juxtaposed and examined eye movement data and reading miscue data to understand how the students processed the verbal and visual parts of the text.

What I Learned

The eye-tracking information revealed clearly that students paid more attention to the print than to the images. Compared to visuals, students fixated more densely on print areas (one fixation per 178 pixels in print area vs. one fixation per 778 pixels in visual area), and the fixations on the print were also generally longer than those on the visual areas (410 vs. 358 ms.) (see Table 9.1). Furthermore, the saccade size (movement from fixation to fixation) was smaller in print than in visual areas (4.51 vs. 6.30 Chinese character spaces). The heat map in Figure 9.2 provides additional evidence of the readers' overall visual attention in this reading event. The print areas, especially the main text and the captions, are generally hotter (darker), showing that readers pay more visual attention and spend more time viewing the print areas. Decorational illustrations are hardly fixated, and neither are some parts of interpretational illustrations.

A closer examination of the eye movements in different print and image areas provides more information about how the students read the multiple representations in this science text. For example, among the three types of print (heading, main text, and caption), headings had the least fixation count

Students' eye movement performances across different text and visual areas

| Interest Area | Area in Pixels | | Fixations | | Ratio | M Fixation | M Saccade |
	No.	% of Total	No.	% of Total	Pixel to Fixation	Duration (ms)	Length (ch sp)
Print							
Main text	91,440	12	598	44.94	153	418	3.87
Headings	34,027	4	103	8.01	330	337	5.43
Captions	23,171	3	133	10.34	174	418	4.24
Total	148,638	19	834	63.29	178	410	4.51
Visual							
Decorational	190,154	24	13	0.97	14,627	307	9.35
Representational	13,514	2	54	3.52	250	380	4.25
Interpretational	92,850	12	314	22.60	296	357	5.29
Total	296,518	38	381	27.09	778	358	6.30
Blank space	341,276	43	124	9.54	2,752	292	9.09

Note. ch sp = character space

Table 9.1: Eye Movement Data for Participants' Readings

Source: Author

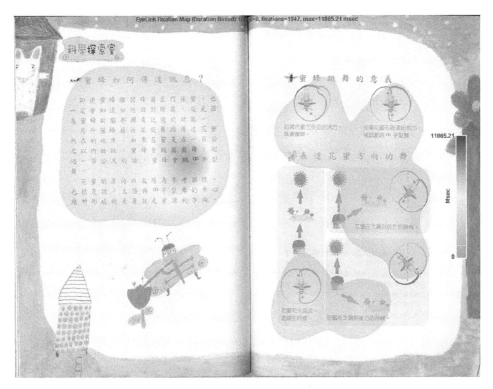

Figure 9.2: Heat Map of Participants' Reading of *Ke xue tong hua 1* [*Science story book series 1*] by C.-G. Hung, 2005)

Sources: Hung, Y.-N. (2014). What are you looking at? An eye movement exploration in science text reading. *International Journal of Science and Mathematics Education, 12*(2), 247.
Original Text: Hung, C.-G. (2005, p. 72). *Ke xue tong hua 1* [*Science story book series 1*]. Taipei: Parenting Source Press, Inc.

(in relation to size) and shortest mean fixation duration. Not one of the six students read aloud all four headings and two of the students read no headings at all. Nevertheless, the most intriguing finding is that while headings were often omitted in the oral reading, students did have some fixations on headings, indicating they "saw" the headings but chose not to read them aloud.

Figure 9.3, for example, shows that Yenyen (pseudonym) made four fixations on this heading, the title of this text, but in her oral reading she omitted it. Yenyen also fixated on several characters in two other headings but did not read them aloud. In other words, the omissions of the headings were not because she didn't look at them but because she chose not to read them aloud. Eye movement information and the recording of oral reading together show that headings are treated differently. Considering the importance of reading

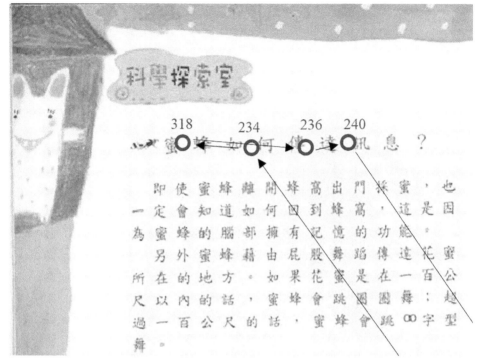

Figure 9.3: Yenyen's Fixations on the Title of the Text From *Ke xue tong hua 1* [*Science story book series 1*] by C.-G. Hung, 2005 in Y.-N. Hung's (2014) Study

Sources: Author. Note: This reader makes four fixations on the title but omits the title in her read aloud. There are no fixations at all on the smaller heading on the top left corner of the page.
Original Text: Hung, C.-G. (2005). *Ke xue tong hua 1* [*Science story book series 1*] (pp. 72–73). Taipei: Parenting Source Press, Inc.

titles and headings to increase comprehension, future research can look at more closely at how titles and headings are processed in the reading process.

Figure 9.3 also shows that there are no fixations at all on the small heading on the top left corner of the page. This title, *Science Exploration Room* (科學探索室), is the name of the section. Section titles received even less attention from the readers. The eye movement data make it clear that the readers did not treat all parts of the text equally.

Among the three types of images (decorational, representational, and interpretational), decorational images had the fewest fixations (in relation to size) and shortest mean fixation duration (see Table 9.1). Decorational images, which contribute very little to the presentation of meaning, made up 24% of the space of this double-page text, but they received only about 1% of fixations. The eye movement data clearly show that readers know where to send their eyes to collect important information for making sense of the text.

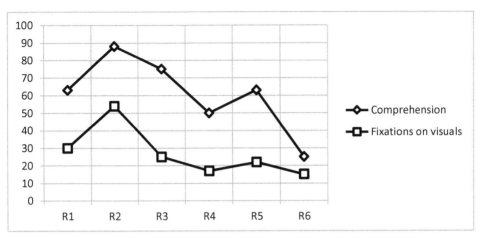

Table 9.2: Comprehension Scores and Percentages of Fixations on Images

Source: Hung, Y.-N. (2014). What are you looking at? An eye movement exploration in science text reading. *International Journal of Science and Mathematics Education, 12*(2), 254.

Miscues and Retellings

Analysis of reading miscues shows that the students' syntactic and semantic acceptability scores for their oral readings were high (both 92%), indicating their concern that their reading made sense and sounded like language (Goodman et al., 2005). I used the readers' retellings to understand their comprehension. Analysis of retellings shows that specific information is what the readers were able to recall and understand the best. All the readers had the general understanding that the sun is used as a reference to find food source, but they couldn't elaborate on how this is done, even though the concepts are visually explained in the interpretational illustrations. This leads me to wonder what the relationship might be between comprehension and the amount of time viewing the illustrations.

As Table 9.2 shows, the higher the students' percentages of fixations on images, the higher their comprehension score. In this study, for example, 88% of Reader 2's fixations landed on image areas and his comprehension score is the highest among the six participants. In contrast, Reader 6 had the fewest fixations on visuals and the lowest comprehension. This EMMA study of science text shows that since text features and images are crucial in reading science text, whether or how much time the readers look at the images is a factor that influences comprehension.

Conclusion

In this chapter I discuss the challenges of reading science text and cite my own EMMA study (Hung, 2014) that involves Taiwanese young readers' reading of a science text rich in print and various visual presentations. In that study I found that readers focus more on the print than on the non-verbal visual representations, showing a word-oriented approach to reading science text. Even though images, illustrations and visual features are important in the representation of contents and meaning, they do not receive the same degree of visual attention, and this is evidenced by the readers' eye movements and oral reading. The EMMA information also shows that titles receive less attention than main text and captions. Most importantly, this study shows that the more a reader looks at the images, the stronger their comprehension.

My colleagues and I had similar findings in another study (Hung, Kuo, & Liao, 2019). In that study, Taiwanese grade-six readers read an English science text that had complex print and visual relationships. Eye movement data showed that even after 12 weeks of science reading comprehension strategy instruction, students still spent more visual attention on print rather than on the multiple visual representations.

The results of EMMA studies using science texts have important implications for science text design and science text reading instruction. Publishers need to develop science text in ways that encourage the reader to use, integrate, and transform information from various types of visual representations. Teachers need to develop more teaching strategies that help students to learn from and with various representations.

This chapter shows the strengths of EMMA as a research method. Eye movement information allows us to understand what the readers are seeing; the oral reading miscue information shows what the readers are thinking while they are reading. Together, EMMA data makes it possible to probe into the dynamic processes of reading, or comprehending in Goodman's term (Goodman, 1996), not just the results of reading, or comprehension. More EMMA research is suggested in order to explore different topics in science reading, such as how readers view, select, or skip different text features and representations in the reading process, how readers integrate information from print and visuals, and effects of different print and visuals layout in promoting optimal processing of multiple representations.

References

Carney, R. N., & Levin, J. R. (2002). Pictorial illustrations still improve students' learning from text. *Educational Psychology Review, 14*(1), 5–26.

Conklin, K., Pellicer-Sánchez, A., & Carrol, G. (2018). *Eye-tracking: A guide for applied linguistics research*. Cambridge: Cambridge University Press.

Duke, N. K. (2000). 3.6 minutes per day: The scarcity of informational texts in first grade. *Reading Research Quarterly, 35*(2), 202–224.

Eilam, B., & Gilbert, J. K. (2014). The significance of visual representations in the teaching of science. In B. Eilam & J. K. Gilbert (Eds.), *Science teachers' use of visual representation* (pp. 3–28). Cham, DK: Springer.

Fang, Z. (2006). The language demands of science reading in middle school. *International Journal of Science Education, 28*(5), 491–520.

Fang, Z. (2008). Going beyond the Fab Five: Helping students cope with the unique linguistic challenges of expository reading in intermediate grades. *Journal of Adolescent and Adult Literacy, 51*(6), 476–487.

Goodman, K. S. (1996). *On reading.* Plymouth, NH: Heinemann.

Goodman, Y. M., Watson, D. J., & Burke, C. L. (2005). *Reading miscue inventory: From evaluation to instruction* (2nd ed.). New York: Richard C. Owen.

Hines, P. J., Wible, B., & McCartney, M. (2010). Learning to read, reading to learn. *Science, 328*, 447.

Hung, C.-G. (2005). *Ke xue tong hua 1 [Science story book series 1].* Taipei: Parenting Source Press, Inc.

Hung, Y.-N. (2014). What are you looking at? An eye movement exploration in science text reading. *International Journal of Science and Mathematics Education, 12*(2), 241–260.

Hung, Y.-N., Kuo, H.-Y., & Liao, S.-C. (2019). Seeing what they see: Elementary EFL students reading science texts. *RELC Journal.* DOI: 10.1177/0033688219854475

Just, M. A., & Carpenter, P. A. (1984). Using eye fixations to study reading comprehension. In D. E. Kieras & M. A. Just (Eds.), *New methods in reading comprehension research* (pp. 151–182). Hillsdale, NJ: Lawrence Erlbaum Associates, Inc.

Moss, B. (2005). Making a case and a place for effective content area literacy instruction in the elementary grades. *Reading Teacher, 59*(1), 46–55.

Levin, J. R. (1981). On functions of pictures in prose. In F. J. Pirozzolo & M. C. Wittrock (Eds.), *Neuropsychological and cognitive processes in reading* (pp. 203–228). New York: Academic.

Paulson E., & Freeman, A. E. (2003). *Insight from the eyes: The science of effective reading* instruction. Portsmouth, NH: Heinemann.

Rayner, K. (1978). Eye movements in reading and information processing. *Psychological Bulletin, 85*, 618–660.

Rayner, K. (1998). Eye movements in reading and information processing: 20 years of research. *Psychological Bulletin, 124*(3), 372–422.

Rayner, K., Chace, K. H., Slattery, T. J., & Ashby, J. (2006). Eye movements as reflections of comprehension processes in reading. *Scientific Studies of Reading, 10*(3), 241–55.

Samuels, S. J., Rasinski, T. V., & Hiebert, E. H. (2011). Eye movements and reading: What teachers need to know. In S. J. Samuels & A. E. Farstrup (Eds.), *What research has to say about reading instruction* (4th ed.) (pp. 25–50). Newark, DE: International Reading Association.

Zwiers, J. (2008). *Building academic language: Essential practices for content classrooms, grades 5-12.* San Francisca, CA: Jossey-Bass.

Part V

Transdisciplinary EMMA Studies

10

Using EMMA to Understand Medical Laboratory Science College Students' Readings of a Disciplinary-Specific Science Text

by Meghan East, D. Jake Follmer, and Koomi J. Kim

Medical Laboratory Science (MLS) is a pre-professional undergraduate program of study combining science and medicine. Practicing MLSs are often found in research centers and clinical settings, such as hospitals, providing much of the objective data used by clinicians in making accurate diagnoses (Forsman, 2002). MLS students, like other college students, often struggle with how to read highly specialized, disciplinary texts (Boakye & Mai, 2016). Despite a common belief that proficient post-secondary students do not need explicit reading instruction, recent work suggests otherwise (Cisco, 2016; Theriault, Matich, Lampi, & Armstrong, 2019). It is important to understand college students current disciplinary reading practices in order to better decipher how to actively engage students in furthering their disciplinary knowledge.

Readers' approaches to understanding text are not universal (Porter, 2018). Rather, readers' engagement often depends on the purpose for reading; the type, structure, and complexity of text; and readers' prior knowledge of text content (Bohn-Gettler & Kendeou, 2014). Correspondingly, research has supported comprehension as discipline specific (Baram-Tsabari & Yarden, 2005), relying on diverse strategies to promote reading comprehension. To successfully engage with and understand complex, disciplinary text, readers need to be able to leverage their developing disciplinary knowledge as well as the use of effective and targeted strategies to make sense of what they read.

Academic languages are often challenging for college students due to variations dependent on discipline. In science, students are expected to know, often without direct instruction, common academic language characteristics: an impersonal authoritative stance, frequent use of nominalizations, disciplinary-specific vocabulary (Snow, 2010), and how to use multimodal aspects such as figures and tables (Lemke, 2004). There is little work examining novice college readers' approaches to comprehending complex scientific text through their developing disciplinary knowledge (Porter, 2018). Similarly, extant work has provided only a limited understanding of readers' enactment of discipline-specific comprehension strategies to support meaning making through reading of complex, multimodal science text. Medical Laboratory Science (MLS) texts are typical of science texts in frequently containing tables, charts, diagrams, pictures, drawings, and formulas. This case study uses eye movement miscue analysis (EMMA) to examine patterns in college readers' reading strategies while engaged with a MLS text. We also explored the roles of readers' use and integration of prior knowledge and multimodal representations in readers' text understanding.

Study Background

Eye Movement Miscue Analysis

We consider reading from both a social-cognitive and social-constructivist framework where readers transact with a text to gain meaning (Paulson, Flurkey, Goodman, & Goodman, 2003) and engage varied strategies in conjunction with prior knowledge to support meaning making from text (Ruddell & Unrau, 2013). Insights into a reader's processing strategies while comprehending (processes occurring during the reading of a text) may be accomplished using miscue analysis (Goodman & Goodman, 2013). Miscues, or unexpected verbal responses during an oral reading, occur due to a reader's linguistic and conceptual cognitive structures, background knowledge, and reading strategies they bring to a literacy event (Goodman, Watson, & Burke, 2005; Paulson, 2002). The more proficient the reader, the more acceptable the final responses they produce as they read. A reader's comprehension, or understanding, is evidenced through a retelling immediately following an oral reading (Goodman & Goodman, 2013).

The additional usage of eye movement tracking during an oral reading (EMMA) enriches miscue analysis (Brown, Kim, & O'Brien Ramirez, 2012; Liwanag, Martens, Martens, & Pelatti, 2017). During an oral reading, it is what the brain processes and reports that is spoken, not just what the eyes see (Goodman & Goodman, 2013). By tracking eye movements, important information is revealed about how a reader interacts with a text to build comprehension and demonstrates the active nature of reading (Brown et al., 2012). Measures of readers' processing, such as fixations, provide key insights into reader strategies to support meaning construction (Liwanag et al., 2017).

Disciplinary Literacy

Disciplinary literacy emphasizes understanding of principles and concepts while engaging in practices standard to a particular field (Fang & Coatoam, 2013). Students need the foundation of literacy skills and disciplinary content in order to develop "social and cognitive practices" (Fang & Coatoam, 2013, p. 628), or habits of mind, that make up a discipline. Further, disciplinary literacy focuses on starting with the discipline and the practices inherently used by experts in the field and adapting literacy practice to support learning (Moje, 2008).

How We Conducted This Study

Readers

Four readers participated in this study and in this chapter we focus on two, Jessica and Cam (pseudonyms). Both were 21 years of age, enrolled as fourth-year college students, identified the United States as their country of birth, and English as their native language. They were enrolled in an advanced hematology course as part of their completion of a MLS major at a mid-sized, public university in the mid-Atlantic United States. The course provided an overview of scientific content related to the text used in this research, the identification of leukemia. When Jessica came in for her reading, she had attended two lectures and one three-hour lab on the topic, while Cam had been absent from the lectures and had not had the lab session. We selected Jessica and Cam as focal participants due to this significant difference in both prior classroom experience and time spent in the lab.

Text

We selected a 960-word expository science text describing the clinical background and hematological case presentation of an 18-month-old patient with acute lymphoblastic leukemia (Ulmer & Larson, 1996). The disciplinary text had 66 sentences presented as two columns of text over three pages. In general, the text was low in narrativity (2.17%ile using Coh-Metrix: Graesser, McNamara, & Kulikowich, 2011) consistent with the dense and informational nature of the content described. It was also low in both concreteness and cohesion, indicating, a large degree of abstract, conceptual terminology with little overlap across concepts and ideas presented in sentences and the text as a whole (Graesser et al., 2011). This was, therefore, a typical science text with an authoritative stance, high lexical density, and many technical terms (Snow, 2010), which is often challenging to those without experience in reading this type of text (Moje, 2008).

The text also contained two tables and three figures, which depicted hematological information to support the case presentation, including example peripheral blood smear composition and select laboratory values. Like the text, these visual representations were informationally dense, contained descriptive captions that referenced critical values and ranges for interpreting hematology parameters, and were presented on each page of the text. Selection of an authentic, disciplinary text with these multimodal features was purposefully done to allow EMMA of the MLS discipline (Goodman et al., 2005).

Three-Part Reading Protocol

A three-part reading protocol was given to all participants. First, prior disciplinary specific knowledge was assessed. Jessica and Cam were asked to describe what they knew about using hematology testing to identify cases of leukemia. Their responses were scored analytically using a conceptual knowledge rubric emphasizing four levels of knowledge: facts and associations (basic; level 1), facts and associations (extended; level 2), concepts and evidence (basic; level 3), and concepts and evidence (extended; level 4) (adapted from Taboada, Tonks, Wigfield, & Guthrie, 2013).

Second, the readers read the text aloud while their eye movements were recorded through an eye tracker. Participants' reading of the authentic, two-column text was self-paced (M reading time=10.3 minutes). For the third part of the reading protocol, the readers were given prompts to examine: their recall of the text (via unaided and aided retellings); their perceived use of tables and figures to help them understand the text; and strategies they used to support their text understanding. We audio recorded and transcribed the readers' responses for analysis. Responses to the retelling prompt were scored in a manner similar to the prior knowledge prompt. Responses to the remaining prompts were scored inductively for themes generated across the readers. After completing the study, participants were shown brief demonstrations of their eye movements during reading of the text.

Eye Tracker

Eye-movement analysis was conducted using the EyeLink 1000 Plus tracker (SR Research) with a desktop mount, a sampling rate of 1,000 Hz, and an estimated accuracy range of 0.25–0.50°. The study was constructed using the Experiment Builder and accompanying Data Viewer. The text was presented on a 22" LCD Dell wide screen monitor with a 1920 x 1080 resolution; participants read the text while positioned 60 cm away from the screen. Prior to reading the first text, participants were familiarized with the eye tracking equipment and were calibrated on their left eye using a 15-point calibration procedure.

EMMA Data Sources

Meghan interviewed each reader using the Burke Reading Interview (BRI) Modified for Older Readers to understand how they identified as a reader and their current beliefs about reading (Goodman et al., 2005). We marked and coded typescripts for each reader using the Classroom Procedure to analyze miscues at the sentence level in relation to the article as a whole (Goodman et al., 2005), and analyzed eye movement data of select miscues. Jessica also completed one retrospective miscue analysis (RMA) session with Meghan after her oral reading to discuss a miscue common to all participants, allowing for a flexible, reader-centered, collaborative dialogue about her reading process to provide additional insight into her work at comprehending (Goodman, Martens, & Flurkey, 2014). Due to the timing of the study in relation to the semester, Jessica was the only reader able to participate in the RMA.

What We Learned

Importance of Readers' Prior Knowledge on Understanding of the Text

Rubric-based scores on the prior knowledge and recall prompts (representing Parts I and III of the reading protocol) are summarized in Table 10.1. The prior knowledge question was a single open-ended question without guidance

	Cam	Jessica
Prior knowledge	1	2
Unaided retelling	1	3
YYN (Strength/No meaning change)	84.1%	84.1%
YYP (Partial strength/ meaning change)	3.2%	6.3%
YYY, YN-, NN- (Meaning change)	12.7%	9.5%

Table 10.1: Scores Obtained on the Prior Knowledge and Retelling Prompts and Sentence Codings From Classroom Procedure Demonstrating Comprehending in Process

Source: Authors.

Note. Scores ranged from 1–4 representing four levels of knowledge from: 1 (facts and limited associations) to 4 (concepts and extended evidence). YYN sentence coding is a strength, indicating no meaning change while reading; YYP is a partial meaning change; YYY, YN-, and NN- all indicate meaning change occurred.

or further clarification from the researchers. Prior to reading the text, Jessica demonstrated understanding that was fact-based and comprised of more limited definitions, not necessarily anchored to the identification of cancer: "We can look at the morphology and use stains to identify, like, what stage or classify them, whether it's the FAB classifications." Cam, having missed the lectures, demonstrated less prior knowledge of the text content, providing few or disparate characteristics of hematology testing in his response: "You put me on the spot . . . you can use different stains to kind of, observe, or confirm what you believe you may have."

Jessica's unaided retelling scores provided evidence of her effective reading comprehension of the text, with a clearer explanation of concepts of hematology testing and some evidence of connections across those concepts: "This young child, I don't remember their gender, but I'm thinking it's a female... they have T-cell ALL, that's uncommon for their age and for being female. I think usually it would be a B-cell ALL, but this one was a T-cell one."

Jessica's aided retelling further supported her in reflecting on the readings and she was able to provide greater detail about the article: "They had to do the hemoglobin manually and take off the buffy coat so then they could get the proper amount...there is a lot of smudge cells on the smear so they had to put bovine albumin on there to prevent that."

This demonstrates the importance of including both unaided and aided retellings as a way to more accurately assess comprehension. Using her prior knowledge, she was able to draw conclusions about the patient described and picked up on the unique patient aspects of this case. Jessica admitted during her BRI (Goodman et al., 2005) that she often struggled with reading and wished she could "stay focused, read every word, and be quicker," showing she not only values but over-relies on the graphophonic language cueing system.

Consistent with scores on the prior knowledge prompt, Cam evidenced understanding of relatively few concepts or characteristics of hematology testing during his retelling: "Umm, it dealt with a girl who, uh, presented with a...uh, she was leukemic...I think it was, umm, a T-cell leukemia." Cam's low comprehension score of 1 from the unaided retelling is interesting when viewed in comparison to his comprehending score of 84.1% using the Classroom Procedure Reader Profile (see Table 10.1). Comprehending scores are derived when looking at each sentence read as the reader produced it, asking if it is syntactically acceptable, semantically acceptable, and whether a meaning change occurred when viewed from the reader's primary language. For example, if Cam produced a sentence exactly as the text was written, it was coded YYN (Y=yes syntactically acceptable, Y=yes semantically acceptable, and N=no meaning change occurred). During his BRI (Goodman et al., 2005) Cam revealed a good reader comprehended the material, but he stressed a difference between performing and understanding. He did not see himself as a good reader, calling himself "lackadaisical." During the retelling, he had an awareness of his insecurity about the topic, stating "Yeah, I just don't want to say something wrong," and limited his own talk. He was acutely aware of his performance while reading, and thus scored similar to Jessica in his comprehending. But his lack of prior knowledge on the subject was revealed by how little he understood at the conclusion of the reading through his sparse retellings.

Readers' Processing and Strategy Use During Reading of the Text

We studied both readers' processing of expository text primarily through examination of the following eye movement data (EyeLink Data Viewer 3.2.1, 2018): dwell time (the sum of durations across all fixations that fell in an area of interest); fixation count (the total number of fixations falling in an interest area); regressions into an interest area (the number of times an interest area was entered from a higher/right-bound interest area); regressions out of an interest area (the number of times an interest area was exited leftward to a lower interest area); and second fixation count (the number of fixations falling in the second run in an interest area). The use of these eye movement metrics as measures of comprehension in reading is established (see key linking assumptions reviewed in Boland, 2004). Analysis of these initial (dwell time and fixation count) and later (regression and second fixation counts) processing measures afforded examination of readers' early processing as well as integration of information from both text and visual representations, respectively.

Summary statistics for select eye movement measures are presented in Table 10.2. These measures provided an indication of the readers' overall processing and integration of both text (at the paragraph level) and visual representations, including both tables and figures across the text, and serve to situate subsequent sentence-level findings obtained through EMMA. Descriptive analysis of the measures revealed that Cam and Jessica processed the text for extended periods of time and with many fixations across interest areas. The readers' processing of the visual representations—including both tables and figures—was comparatively less than their processing of the text. Jessica fixated to a greater degree on both tables and figures than Cam (and the other two readers). Cam referred to the tables and figures less than Jessica, and the ratio of his fixations to the total time he spent processing them suggests that he sampled the representations quickly and with little depth. Jessica did read the captions below the figures.

		Cam	Jessica
Processing of text			
Dwell time[a]		448.33 sec	468.06 sec
Fixation count:	Total	1424	1583
Processing of visual representations			
Dwell time[a]		25.79 sec	93.64 sec
Fixation count:	Total	87	292
Integration of text and visual representations			
Regression into representations: Count: Total		11	17
Regression out of representations: Count: Total		3	9
Second representation fixation count: Total		32	155

Table 10.2: Summary Statistics for Select Eye Movement Measures

Source: Authors.

Note. Statistics representing eye movement measures were summed across interest areas to provide indexes of readers' processing across text and visual representations. Eye movement measures representation text processing are based on paragraph-level interest areas. For ease of interpretation, dwell time was converted to seconds.

Descriptive analyses of readers' integration of text and all visual representations containing disciplinary specific information, revealed additional, unique findings. Readers' regressions into and out of the visual representations were comparable. Both had more regressions into than out of the representations (see Table 10.2), which suggest a similar degree of strategic processing of representations to support meaning construction. Jessica and Cam moved similarly back-and-forth between text and multimodal representations of figures and tables to help their developing disciplinary specific understanding.

Jessica's and Cam's second fixations across all figures and tables showed greater variability (see Table 10.2). Consistent with the total fixation-based findings, Jessica demonstrated considerably more second fixations of visual representations (155 fixations, compared to Cam's 32 fixations), indicating intentional and additional processing of the figures and tables to support meaning making, while Cam failed to navigate them efficiently as evidenced in part by his lower retelling score.

Analysis of the two readers' unaided and aided retellings revealed a number of findings regarding their perceived use of representations and strategies to help them understand the text. Cam reported he did not leverage the representations to help him understand the text. Jessica indicated sporadic use of the representations to support her developing disciplinary specific understanding of the case presentation and specific laboratory results.

With respect to reported use of strategies during reading, Cam indicated limited use of strategies to augment their text understanding. Cam reported rereading in the event his understanding broke down, which is not as effective in supporting long-term retention of textual information (Dunlosky, Rawson, Marsh, Nathan, & Willingham, 2013). Conversely, Jessica reported leveraging her developing disciplinary specific knowledge to support her text understanding; elaboration and integration with prior knowledge during reading has been shown to support the development of disciplinary specific knowledge-based inferences (McNamara & Magliano, 2009).

EMMA: Understanding Readers' Miscues

In listening to and analyzing the oral readings from Jessica and Cam, we found a high percentage of high-quality miscues to demonstrate language strength (Goodman et al., 2005). A statistical analysis revealed both Jessica and Cam were transacting efficiently with the text (see Table 10.1), as shown, for example, by both readers having the majority of sentences produced having no meaning change (YYN) or only a partial or minor meaning change (YYP): Jessica 90.4% and Cam 87.3%. Select areas of interest were chosen for analysis as they revealed disciplinary-specific miscues of the two readers.

Interestingly, both Jessica and Cam omitted the abbreviations in parentheses (RBC and Hb) from this sentence: *The platelet count, red blood cell count (RBC), hemoglobin (Hb), and hematocrit were critically low* (original). Jessica and Cam chose to read text (both words and abbreviations) contained in the parentheses for other sentences, but not on a consistent basis. Cam would often read the text found in the parentheses quietly, almost as if to himself. The purposeful omissions in this sentence were interesting to note for the discipline. Jessica and Cam had already become acclimated towards a laboratory culture, where it is standard practice in the MLS field to use the abbreviations "RBC" for red blood cell and "Hb" for hemoglobin in writing, but when speaking, such abbreviations may not be used. This omission demonstrates how the students are beginning to exhibit discipline-specific conventions of the field. Later in the text when confronted with these abbreviations, Jessica and Cam demonstrated their ability to use discipline-specific knowledge by consciously choosing to substitute *red blood cells* (miscue) and *hemoglobin* (miscue). In general, their eye movements showed both readers not only looked at the omitted text in parentheses, but later at the abbreviations when they spoke the full words, showing their comfort for how each should be spoken based on their disciplinary knowledge.

Another example (see Figure 10.1) of the students utilizing their burgeoning disciplinary knowledge is in the multiple complex miscues that occurred across all readers in the following sentence: *The patient was given an exchange transfusion to raise her RBC count to 3.0 X 10¹²/L, her Hb to 107 g/L, and her hematocrit to 0.30* (original, Ulmer & Larson, 1996, p. 720). The text they read (Ulmer & Larson, 1996) presented patient results in a European fashion, while they are familiar with writing units following an American standardized way. In the U.S., units for hemoglobin are typically written as g/dL (grams per deciliter) and values often fall around 15 in healthy individuals. The text used the European way of writing this value, which these readers were not as familiar with, grams per liter (g/L), and values would be 10-fold higher: 150 g/L. When the text read *her Hb to 107 g/L* (original), each reader paused (Jessica six seconds and Cam three seconds), expecting to see a value around 15 after the Hb. This pause was significant, showing Jessica and Cam were presumably working to construct meaning from the text, attempting to reconcile the reported value and units within their schema (Duckett, 2003). They were using various socio-cognitive strategies while transacting with the text in an effort to comprehend.

Eye movements during the pause showed how Jessica sampled, made disciplinary-specific predictions, and regressed, before moving slowly through the text. This demonstrates how she was comprehending the text, or making sense, in process (see Figure 10.1). She had 17 fixation points over six words with an average fixation duration of 512 milliseconds. This series of short saccades with multiple regressions suggests Jessica used her disciplinary knowledge to slow down her reading, make a prediction, disconfirm, regress, and confirm the text in an effort to build confidence in her understanding (Paulson, 2002). Jessica

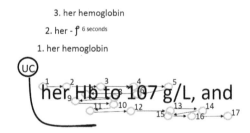

Figure 10.1: Marked Typescript With Eye Movement Fixations

Source: Authors.

Note: Underlining shows words included in miscue, UC=Uncorrected Miscue; above line text are oral miscues made by Jessica; the circles represent Jessica's multiple eye fixations numbered in sequence, the arrows show saccades between fixations (Ulmer & Larson, 1996, p. 720).

was using all cueing systems (syntactic, semantic, graphophonic) with her developing discipline-specific knowledge. In her retelling she acknowledged using her background knowledge of terminology to predict what was going to be said. During her brief RMA session, she laughed when she heard herself: "I definitely don't see it as being 107. I'm guessing it should be 10.7." She further remarked that the units were "weird." As a novice in the discipline, she has not yet developed fluency in unit conversion. Cam made a similar pause of three seconds between *her* and *Hb*, but chose to read <H> <b> as it was written. This shorter pause and usage of *Hb* indicate that he was not as familiar with the term. As noted, when speaking in the profession, Hb would be referenced as hemoglobin. If Cam was using his background knowledge to comprehend in process he would have read "hemoglobin" here instead of Hb. This would have been an excellent sentence to review with Cam during an RMA to learn more about his thought process and work at comprehension.

EMMA: Readers' Processing of Visual Representations

The structure of this text was complicated. Often in the discipline, there are many complex ideas with frequent references to tables, figures, charts, and diagrams (Lemke, 2004). Readers need to be able to use the visual references to help support and enrich the textual elements of reading to build understanding (Hung, 2013). In the following sentence, Jessica and Cam were able to produce a syntactically and semantically correct sentence with no change in meaning: *Results of laboratory tests taken on admission are displayed in Table 1* (original, Ulmer & Larson, 1996, p. 720).

Here the text references Table 1 for laboratory values, but Table 1 was on the following page of text and not visible on the screen to the reader. Cam's eye movements show he looked at the two figures on the bottom of the page at the reference and then moved back in to the text to continue reading. Interestingly, at the textual reference, Jessica did not look at the images, but when she finished reading the page, she did look at the images and read the captions out loud. A limitation of this study was that the readers were unable to flip between pages to utilize tables and figures when referenced, and both Jessica and Cam mentioned this difficulty during the retelling. They tried to utilize the visual information across the three pages to support meaning (Kress & van Leeuwen, 2006), but frequently found the placement of visual representations to not be helpful and chose to abandon them in their meaning-making process.

Conclusions: What College Educators Need to Consider

The current findings are interpreted against the backdrop where these college readers are socially and cognitively developing in the MLS discipline. Their eye movements while reading show they were working hard (Duckett, 2003) at making meaning and highlight the use and importance of their developing discipline-specific background knowledge. They utilized many strategies common to reading across disciplines: scanning, predicting, inferring, confirming/disconfirming, integrating, and correcting (Goodman et al., 2005).

Jessica and Cam were at opposite ends of the spectrum in terms of their background knowledge on the topic read. Jessica had approximately six hours more of classroom and laboratory experience than Cam. They had taken the same MLS courses in previous semesters and had similar experiences in hematology. The key difference here was their exposure on leukemias through the classroom and laboratory. The importance on drawing from their background knowledge in understanding a complex, multimodal disciplinary text was evident in the differences in their comprehension scores and retellings. Jessica was able to frequently reference facts important for the discipline and made associations and connections across the reading with her own experiences. At the college-level, when students are preparing for entrance into a profession, their active participation in learning disciplinary topics enables them to apply their knowledge to future experiences.

The layout and construction of a text is vitally important; if figures and tables are to be used to support and enrich comprehension, they must be both accessible and leveraged by readers (Kress & van Leeuwen, 2006). We found Jessica and Cam attempted to utilize the visual representations to enrich their understanding, but also noted considerable variability across their access to and use of such representations to bolster their comprehension processes. In some ways, this finding bears on the difficulty inherent in examining readers' integration across multi-page text and representations using eye-tracking methodologies. This finding is significant not only in light of our interest in how readers use visual representations, but also as an important consideration for future eye movement studies. Jessica and Cam, even at the college-level, should be guided explicitly on integrating representations with text to augment their comprehension processes, especially given the frequency which they occur in a disciplinary science text. When planning eye movement studies regarding integration of visual information, it is likewise important for the image to be readily accessible to the reader.

Discipline-specific teaching implications include the importance of authentic experiences and practice in the field of MLS as a means to create the habits of mind for the profession. The teaching of socio-cognitive reading strategies for the discipline should be made explicit, highlighting how students can build understanding from their existing schema. Educators need to help students become aware of their background knowledge as a building block for future learning, and be taught how to leverage it when reading. Authentic and meaningful text should be provided to support the development of novice readers' disciplinary literacy. In the MLS field, this means incorporating actual case studies from the literature that tie together classroom material, lab values, and visual images of testing performed. If students' only transaction with disciplinary texts comes from textbooks, they lose out on guided practice reading from professional journals used upon graduation. These disciplinary-specific texts often are quite multimodal, and students need direct instruction on how to navigate these texts. Making these practices explicit is likely to ease students' development in a discipline.

References

Baram-Tsabari, A., & Yarden, A. (2005). Text genre as a factor in the formation of scientific literacy. *Journal of Research in Science Teaching, 42*(4), 403–428.

Boakye, N., & Mai, M. (2016). A needs analysis for a discipline-specific reading intervention. *English Language Teaching, 9*(3), 235-247. doi:10.5539/elt.v9n3p235

Bohn-Gettler, C. M., & Kendeou, P. (2014). The interplay of reader goals, working memory, and text structure during reading. *Contemporary Educational Psychology, 39*(3), 206–219.

Boland, J. E. (2004). Linking eye movements to sentence comprehension in reading and listening. In M. Carreiras & C. Clifton Jr. (Eds.), *The on-line study of sentence comprehension: Eyetracking, ERP, and beyond* (pp. 51–76). New York: Psychology Press.

Brown, J., Kim, K., & O'Brien Ramirez, K. (2012). What a teacher hears, what a reader sees: Eye movements from a phonics-taught second grader. *Journal of Early Childhood Literacy, 12*(2), 202–222.

Cisco, J. (2016). A case study of university honors students in humanities through a disciplinary literacy lens. *Literacy Research and Instruction, 55*(1), 1–23. https://doi.org/10.1080/19388071.2015.1063742

Duckett, P. (2003). Envisioning story: The eye movements of beginning readers. *Literacy Teaching and Learning, 7*(1–2), 77–89.

Dunlosky, J., Rawson, K. A., Marsh, E. J., Nathan, M. J., & Willingham, D. T. (2013). Improving students' learning with effective learning techniques: Promising directions from cognitive and educational psychology. *Psychological Science in the Public Interest, 14*(1), 4–58.

EyeLink Data Viewer 3.2.1 [Computer software]. (2018). Mississauga, Ontario, Canada: SR Research Ltd.

Fang, Z, and Coatoam, S. (2013). Disciplinary literacy: What you want to know about it. *Journal of Adolescent & Adult Literacy, 56*(8), 627–632.

Forsman, R. W. (2002). The value of the laboratory professional in the continuum of care. *Clinical Leadership & Management Review, 16*(6), 370–373.

Goodman, Y., & Goodman, K. (2013). To err is human: Learning about language processes by analyzing miscues. In D. Alvermann, N. Unrau, & R. Ruddall (Eds.), *Theoretical models and processes of reading* (6th edition, pp. 525–543). Newark, DE: International Reading Association.

Goodman, Y., Martens, P., and Flurkey, A. (2014). *The essential RMA: A window into readers' thinking*. Katonah, NY: Richard C. Owen Publishers, Inc.

Goodman, Y., Watson, D., and Burke, C. (2005). *Reading miscue inventory: From evaluation and instruction*. Katonah, NY: Richard C. Owen Publishing.

Graesser, A. C., McNamara, D. S., & Kulikowich, J. M. (2011). Coh-metrix: Providing multilevel analyses of text characteristics. *Educational Researcher, 40*(5), 223–234.

Hung, Y.-N. (2013). "What are you looking at?" An eye movement exploration in science text reading. *International Journal of Science and Mathematics Education, 12*, 241–260.

Kress, G., and van Leeuwen, T. (2006). *Reading images: The grammar of visual design.* New York: Routledge.

Lemke, J. L. (2004). The literacies of science. In E. W. Saul (Ed.), *Crossing borders in literacy and science instruction: Perspectives on theory and practice* (pp. 33–47). Newark, DE: International Reading Association.

Liwanag, M., Martens, P., Martens, R., & Pelatti, C. 2017. Examining a reader's meaning-making process of picture books using eye movement miscue analysis. *Literacy Research: Theory, Method, and Practice, 66*(1), 248–263. https://doi.org/10.1177/2381336917719256

McNamara, D. S., & Magliano, J. P. (2009). Towards a comprehensive model of comprehension. In B. Ross (Ed.), *The psychology of learning and motivation* (pp. 297–384). New York: Elsevier Science.

Moje, E. (2008). Foregrounding the disciplines in secondary literacy teaching and learning: A call for change. *Journal of Adolescent & Adult Literacy, 52*(2), 96–107.

Paulson, E. (2002). Are oral reading word omissions and substitutions caused by careless eye movements? *Reading Psychology, 23*, 45–66.

Paulson, E., Flurkey, A., Goodman, Y., & Goodman, K. (2003). Eye movements and miscue analysis: Reading from a constructivist perspective. In *The fifty–second yearbook of the National Reading Conference* (pp. 343–355). Oak Creek, Wisconsin: National Reading Conference, Inc.

Porter, H. (2018). *Co-constructing undergraduate disciplinary literacy: A case study of disciplinary communities.* (Doctoral dissertation). Available from ProQuest Dissertations & Theses Global. (2234198549).

Ruddell, R. B. & Unrau, N. J. (2013). Reading as a motivated meaning-construction process: The reader, the text, and the teacher. In D. Alvermann, N. Unrau, & R. Ruddall (Eds.), *Theoretical models and processes of reading.* (6th edition, pp. 1015–067). Newark, DE: International Reading Association.

Snow, C. (2010). Academic language and the challenge of reading for learning about science. *Science, 328*, 450–452.

Taboada, A., Tonks, S. M., Wigfield, A., & Guthrie, J. T. (2013). Effects of motivational and cognitive variables on reading comprehension. In D. Alvermann, N. Unrau, & R. Ruddall (Eds.), *Theoretical models and processes of reading.* (6th ed., pp. 589–610). Newark, DE: International Reading Association.

Theriault, J., Matich, L., Lampi, J., & Armstrong, S. (2019). The continued need for strategy investigations: College readers' use of PILLAR. *Journal of Adolescent & Adult Literacy, 62*(5), 541–549. doi:10.1002/jaal.925

Ulmer, L., & Larson, L. (1996). Clinical pathology rounds: Acute lymphoblastic leukemia. *Laboratory Medicine, 27*(11), 720–722.

11

Case Study Exploring an International College Student's Reading for Academic Purposes Using Eye Movement Miscue Analysis (EMMA)

by Yang Wang and Ismahan Arslan-Ari

Every year thousands of international students study for higher education degrees in the United States (Institute of International Education, 2017). Many international students who do not speak English as their native language struggle with reading and learning in their discipline. College learning usually involves intense reading (Nist & Simpson, 2000); however, many students do not learn how to read academic texts in high school or college.

Academic reading is reading a text and learning for an educational purpose (Isakson & Isakson, 2017). It requires "reading proficiency, knowledge of reading strategies to use as needed, motivation to persist in reading, and the metacognitive awareness to recognize if reading goals are being met and what to do about it if not" (Isakson & Isakson, 2017, p. 157). Many international students need support in reading in their disciplines when they are adjusting to living in a new place and communicating primarily in a second language.

Previous studies find college English learners use their first language reading strategies in English reading, rely more on the linguistic systems, use more graphophonic information and test-taking strategies, translate, and switch codes (Li, 1992; Wang, 2014, 2019; Wang & Gilles, 2017). Readers who have stronger metacognitive awareness often select more effective strategies and better monitor their comprehension (Zhang & Wu, 2009). However, few studies have looked into international students' reading process when they read academic text with figures and provided implications. This study explores how an international student approaches academic reading. It examines this question: What does eye movement miscue analysis (EMMA) reveal about an international graduate student's reading of academic text with figures?

constructive

Theoretical Framework

Reading is the transaction between the reader and the text to construct meaning (Rosenblatt, 1978). When reading, readers draw on the syntactic, semantic, graphophonic, and pragmatic cueing systems (context or situation), their prior knowledge, and their cultural backgrounds to make meaning (Y. Goodman, Watson, & Burke, 2005; Moore & Gilles, 2005). Readers' prior experiences and purposes in reading influence their reading processes when they read for learning (McKenna & Robinson, 2014). Readers also use cognitive strategies in their transaction with the text: they initiate reading, sample and select information, infer and predict, confirm or disconfirm, correct, integrate, and terminate (K. Goodman, 1994).

Built on a socio-psycholinguistic framework, miscue analysis provides a window to explore readers' reading process (Y. Goodman et al., 2005). A miscue is a reader's varied response from the expected response when reading. The hybrid form of Eye Movement Miscue Analysis (EMMA) (Paulson, 2000) examines the reader's reading process using both miscue analysis and eye movements (more explanation is found in Chapter 3). EMMA research (Paulson & Goodman, 2008) has demonstrated that readers fixate between 50% and 80% of the words in a text. Text difficulty, the reader's proficiency and purpose, and other factors affect the fixation rate (Paulson & Goodman, 2008). Research also demonstrates that reading is not a linear process; that eye movements and miscues and the relationship between them reveal the process of comprehending and readers' comprehension; and that reading is a constructivist art (Paulson & Freeman, 2003). English-as-a-Foreign-Language readers focus more on the written text than the visuals when they read science texts, and they understand more when they refer to the visuals (Hung, 2014; Hung, Kuo, & Liao, 2019).

Most academic texts include a variety of visuals, such as graphics, charts, and maps. Recent research focuses on the use of written text and visuals to construct meaning (Unsworth, 2004). Studies show that readers learn better when information is presented with text and image and builds on their prior knowledge (Feathers & Arya, 2015; Mayer, 2009). Effective comprehension relies on "meaningful integrative connections between verbal and graphical features" (Mason, Tornatora, & Pluchino, 2013, p. 96).

Several studies (Feathers & Arya, 2015; Mason et al., 2013, 2015; Mason, Scheiter, & Tornatora, 2017) using eye movements found that readers make integrative transitions between text and images. The integrative transition is the number of times in which the learner's eye fixation moves from a text segment to the image or from the image to a text segment, reflecting the learner's attempt to integrate text and visual elements (Johnson & Mayer, 2012). While texts express meaning through language cueing systems, images have graphical cueing systems to create meaning, such as color, and shape (Liwanag, Pelatti, Martens, & Martens, 2016). Meaning construction occurs through readers' transaction with visual and verbal signs, and it is guided by the social context (Goodman, 1996).

What We Did

This mixed methods case study (Stake, 1995) used both qualitative and quantitative data to provide an in-depth understanding about how an international student who speaks English as a second language reads academic text with figures. We collected the quantitative data (numbers of miscues, eye movements) and qualitative data (reading, retelling, and eye movement) concurrently.

Our reader, Yutong, was a new graduate student in education. Yutong was from Mainland China and earned her K-12 education and bachelor's and master's degrees in translation and interpretation there. She had lived in the United States for a year at the time of this study. In a previous interview, Yutong reported that "reading in English is learning," indicating her purpose for reading was learning.

Yutong believed that she needed to read and improve her English language proficiency from reading academic materials. She also mentioned that once she achieved language proficiency, she could read for pleasure. When Yutong met something that she did not know, she looked it up in Google or Wikipedia. She read four academic essays per day in her independent reading time to improve her reading speed as well as to prepare for the language exams in China.

We selected two academic texts based on Yutong's interest and background for her to read. To ensure the text features were similar to the academic materials that she read, both texts included in-text citations and figures that were diagrams as a supplementary explanation of the content. We decided on a book and a dissertation; however, both texts were lengthy, so we selected a section from each. Each section we selected included a diagram along with text and could be understood without the context of the entire book or dissertation. Each section was also about 630 words, which was long enough to allow us to observe Yutong's meaning-making processes and document and analyze her miscues.

Collecting the Data

We displayed a double-page spread of the text on a monitor so we could track her eye movements. The two texts were "Possible Outcomes of Intercultural Encounters" (referred as "Intercultural Encounters," a section from a chapter in *Intercultural Learning in the Classroom* (Fennes & Hapgood, 1997) and "Cognitive Theory of Multimedia Learning" (referred as "Multimedia Learning"), a section from Arslan-Ari's (2013) dissertation, *Examining the Effects of Cueing and Prior Knowledge on Learning, Mental Effort, and Study Time in a Complex Animation*. Both texts covered two pages with the diagram in the middle of each page. The diagram in "Intercultural Encounters" showed the flow of different phases in the adjustment cycle. The diagram in "Multimedia Learning" presented how learners engage in the cognitive process. For each text, we displayed the same diagram on both pages to capture the eye movement between it and the text. The text difficulty according to the Lexile Analyzer was 1200L to 1300L, which is considered college reading level. The average sentence length was approximately 20 words.

We conducted two reading sessions with Yutong. Each session lasted about one hour. First, Yutong browsed the text and shared the prior knowledge she had about the topic. Then she read aloud independently. After each reading, Yutong did a retelling and answered questions. The two retelling evaluation guides were modified from the miscue analysis retelling summary of nonfiction text (Y. Goodman et al., 2005) and created based on the specific information, the generalizations, and the major concepts that the reader recalled and understood. We also took notes on Yutong's inferences, use of the visual aid, strategy use, and other aspects of the reading process.

Yutong's eye movements were recorded using the Tobii Pro X3-120 portable screen-based eye tracker with a sampling rate of 120 Hz. First, Yutong's eyes were calibrated in order to track and gather her eye movements. After the calibration, Yutong read aloud the texts on the screen while the eye tracker recorded her eye movement simultaneously. The Tobii Pro Studio software was used to replay and analyze the eye movements.

Analyzing the Data

All the reading and retelling data were video-recorded and transcribed for analysis. We marked Yutong's miscues on the typescript and used the in-depth procedure of miscue analysis (Y. Goodman et al., 2005) to analyze her miscues and retellings. Each miscue was analyzed at the sentence level and in the entire text for syntactic acceptability, semantic acceptability, meaning change, and graphophonic similarity.

Eye movement data analysis started with determining Areas of Interests (AOIs) for text and image (diagram) and the total fixation duration and total fixation counts for each AOIs in Tobii Pro Studio. We also examined Yutong's eye movements to find the patterns and calculate the integrative transitions. Integrative transitions were computed by summing the number of times the eye fixation moved from the text to the diagram and from diagram to text. Integrative transitions reflect the reader's attempts to integrate text and image (Mason et al., 2013). A gaze plot, which show the location, order, and duration of the fixations on the screen (Tobii Pro, 2020), was analyzed to understand the reader's reading patterns. Fixation points and saccades were also examined to deepen the participants' reading behaviors. (See Chapter 3 for explanations.)

What We Learned

Miscue Analysis

Table 11.1 shows that Yutong's reading demonstrated her strong focus on meaning construction and grammatical relations (that her reading sounded like language) as she read. The combined percentage of "no loss" and "partial loss" is 84.2% for "Intercultural Encounters" and 96% for "Multimedia Learning." The combined percentage of "strength" and "partial strength" is 79% for "Intercultural Encounters" and 100% for "Multimedia Learning." The high graphic and sound similarity percentages (100% for "Intercultural Encounters" and 93.3% for "Multimedia Learning") of her word substitutions indicate that her miscues looked and sounded highly similar to what was in the texts. However, her retelling scores of 55% ("Intercultural Encounters") and 60% ("Multimedia Learning") (see Table 11.1) show that her comprehension of the two pieces was not as strong. Those data, in addition to only making three or four miscues per hundred words in both texts, suggest Yutong may have focused more on surface accuracy than meaning-making, and she con-

	Miscue per hundred words	Meaning Construction (percentages)			Grammatical Relations (percentages)				Word Substitution (percentages)						Retelling (%)	Eye Movement			
									Graphic similarity			Sound similarity							
		No Loss	Partial Loss	Loss	Strength	Partial Strength	Over-correction	Weakness	High	Some	None	High	Some	None		Fixations	Text Fixation Duration	Image Fixation Duration	Integrative Transition
Intercultural Encounters	3	68.4	15.8	15.8	73.7	5.3	10.5	10.5	100	0	0	100	0	0	55	793	276.8 seconds	21.9 seconds	14
Multimedia Learning	4	84	12	4	96	4	0	0	93.3	6.7	0	93.3	6.7	0	60	994	258.9 seconds	34.9 seconds	38

Table 11.1: Miscue Analysis and Eye Movement of the Two Selected Texts
Source: Authors.

centrated more on coding the smaller units of the texts than synthesizing and understanding the entire texts.

Yutong reported that she had prior knowledge about the topic in "Intercultural Encounters" when she browsed it before reading aloud; however, she did not connect the text to her prior knowledge when she retold. Though she reported "Multimedia Learning" was more difficult and she had little prior knowledge, her retelling shows she understood it better than "Intercultural Encounters." Additionally, Yutong connected "Multimedia Learning" to her experiences by using the cognitive model to explain her field observation. The connection was that she, as a volunteer at a bilingual elementary school, observed that the classroom teacher used multiple ways to engage the children in learning new knowledge. Yutong's connection from the text to her practicing experience supported her stronger understanding of this text.

Eye Movement

Yutong made a total of 793 fixations for "Intercultural Encounters" and 994 fixations for "Multimedia Learning" (see Table 11.1). A sample eye movement recording can be found at https://youtu.be/n1gl0hGkY7M. In the recording, red dots show Yutong's fixations and the size of the dots indicate her fixation duration. As seen in the eye movement recording, she did not fixate on every item in the text in her oral reading. Also, her fixations did not follow in consecutive order from left to right. Her eyes occasionally regressed, going back to previous text. The fixations indicate Yutong's non-linear and dynamic meaning-making process.

Eye Movement Miscue Analysis

Yutong made mainly two types of miscues across the two texts—substitutions and omissions. Below, we discuss her substitutions, corrections of some miscues, dialect miscues, and omissions.

Yutong made substitutions for text on which she did not fixate. When she read "Intercultural Encounters," she fixated on 10 out of 11 (90%) text items for which she made substitutions. She made eight regressions out of those 11 miscues and read on. For instance, her eyes fixated on *different* in *a different culture* when she read it as "difficult." Her eyes regressed and she corrected that miscue because it did not make sense.

In "Multimedia Learning," Yutong fixated on all the seven text items for which she made substitutions and regressed on six of them. For instance, her eyes fixated on *internal* in *building internal connections* when she read aloud "international." Her eyes regressed and she corrected right away. The miscues for which she confirmed and continued reading without regressing did not change the meaning in both texts. For example, she read "gets to" for *gets into* in *which gets into the WM*.

We used gaze plots to show Yutong's eye movements while reading the text aloud (see Figure 11.1). The round dots show Yutong's fixations and the size of the dots indicate her fixation duration, with larger dots indicating longer duration and smaller dots less. Also, the numbers outside the dots show the sequence of those fixations. The gaze plot for "Intercultural Encounters" is in Figure 11.1. As seen in Figure 11.1, the text Yutong did not fixate on included *a*, *of*, *not*, and *in* (see the recording of this vignette at https://youtu.be/c-I41Mg_U3w). Her eye movements show that although she read the text aloud without any miscues, her eyes did not fixate on each text item.

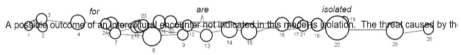

Figure 11.1: Eye Movement Patterns for Yutong's Miscues in "Intercultural Encounters"

Source: Authors.
Source: Fennes, H., & Hapgood, K. (1997, p. 31). *Intercultural learning in the classroom.* London & Washington: Cassell.

Yutong did not fixate on *of* when she substituted "for" in the phrase of *A possible outcome of an intercultural encounter*. She used her semantic and syntactic knowledge to predict a preposition without fixating on what followed *A possible outcome*. Then she predicted "an intercultural encounter are not indicated" by inserting "are," relying on her semantic and syntactic knowledge. At the end of the sentence, she again integrated her knowledge of language and the text to predict "is isolated." Fixation point #20 shows she spent more time on *isolation* and then her eyes regressed to *intercultural encounter* to reread and reconfirm her understanding before she continued to read the next sentence.

Yutong corrected five out of 11 miscue substitutions in "Intercultural Encounters" and five out of seven substitutions in "Multimedia Learning." Whenever she corrected a miscue, her eyes fixated on the text and regressed.

Figure 11.2: Eye Movement Patterns for Yutong's Correction of "Cultural" for *Culture* **in "Intercultural Encounters"**

Source: Authors.
Source: Fennes, H., & Hapgood, K. (1997, p. 31). *Intercultural learning in the classroom.* London & Washington: Cassell.

When she miscued, she at times fixated longer on the text and regressed in an attempt to correct. Figure 11.2 is an example of Yutong correcting one miscue. In Figure 11.2, she read *culture shock* as "cultural shock" and her eye movement shows that she looked back at the word of *culture* and attempted to correct it (see the recording of this vignette at https://youtu.be/GpTAG2A1k2c). Her initial substitution "cultural" did not change the meaning of the text; however, she corrected it.

Yutong's dialect miscues reflect her linguistic background and do not affect her meaning-making. For instance, Yutong omitted the -s ending for the plural forms of nouns, such as instruction(s), row(s), and image(s). Her missing -s ending during her oral reading was because there was no -s ending marker in her first language. Yutong made two dialect miscues in "Intercultural Encounters" and eight in "Multimedia Learning." She fixated on all her dialect miscues in both texts and barely made regressions from the dialect miscues to other texts or from other texts to the dialect miscues.

Yutong omitted text on which she did not fixate and text that she did. Two out of the six (33%) omissions in "Intercultural Encounters" and seven out of ten (70%) omissions in "Multimedia Learning" were fixation points. Most of the omissions are the citation and descriptive text and did not change the meaning. For example, she omitted "*e.g. for a term or for a school year,*" "*see Figure 6,*" "*CTML,*" and "*Mayer, 2009.*" She did not correct any of those omissions and her eyes only regressed for two out of the 16 omissions (13%) reading two texts. For example, Yutong did not fixate on the word *the* before *teacher* in the sentence of *such a pupil will seek to stay with the classmates or the teacher.* This omission of *the* did not change the meaning of the text. Her eyes did not regress, and she continued reading without correcting. Yutong's only omission that resulted in meaning change was *Resolution* in "Intercultural Encounters." Her eye movement recording (which can be found at https://youtu.be/n1gl0hGkY7M) shows that she did not fixate on it. Her retelling reflected missing the information about the phase of "resolution." Missing this last phase of the adjustment cycle impacted her understanding of the complete adjusting process.

Integrative Transitions Between Texts and Images

In both texts, Yutong focused more on the texts than on the diagrams. The fixation duration on the text was 276.8 seconds (92.7 %) and on the diagram 21.9 seconds (7.3%) for "Intercultural Encounters." The fixation duration on the text is 258.9 seconds (88.1%) and 34.9 seconds (11.9%) for "Multimedia Learning." Although we observed the similar patterns in both texts, she focused on the diagram more frequently in "Multimedia Learning." The reason might be that the diagram in "Multimedia Learning" was more complicated; meanwhile, Yutong reported "Multimedia Learning" was harder to understand. When she had a difficult time understanding the content, she checked the diagram for more information and to make connections.

Yutong made transitions between the text and diagram. In total, she made four integrative transitions from the text to the diagram and ten from the diagram to the text when she read "Intercultural Encounters." She made 30 integrative transitions from the text to the diagram and eight from the diagram to the text when she read "Multimedia Learning." Those integrative transitions reflect her attempts to integrate the text and visual information to support meaning construction. Sample recording of her integrative transition can be seen at https://youtu.be/nHXyjbZN0v8.

Yutong made more integrative transitions toward the end of the sentences than in the beginning or in the middle of those sentences. She transitioned to the diagrams where the texts introduced new terms or when she read keywords that are included in the diagram. Her eyes did not transition to the diagrams when she miscued. When she read "Multimedia Learning," she paused after the first page and spent time studying the diagram. This demonstrates how she actively sought information during that silent moment.

We observed Yutong's reading flow (Flurkey, 2008) varied when reading different sections of the texts. She read slowly and the fixation duration was longer when the text and diagram became challenging for her and when she made more transitions between the text and diagram. She read quickly and the fixation duration was shorter when the text was easy for her to understand. Yutong's fixation stayed closer along with the text line by line in the beginning, and her fixation patterns became more dynamic when she read further into the text and when she read challenging sections and relied on the image for understanding.

Discussion

Reading for academic purposes in English as a second language is a nonlinear process. Yutong did not fixate on every text item when she read and the duration of her fixations varied. This supports findings from the previous studies in eye movement (Paulson & Freeman, 2003; Paulson & Goodman, 2008). Additionally, Yutong looked at the texts, images, and margin areas and transitioned between the texts and images to deepen her understanding. Those transitions have no correlations with her miscues. She fixated on most substituted texts and skipped many in-text citations for efficiency when she became familiar with the texts.

Yutong used all the language cueing systems to make meaning when she read for academic purposes in her second language. Her miscue analysis scores (see Table 11.1) and her EMMA analyses together reflect her using multiple cues in the texts to construct meaning. When the text became challenging, besides drawing on the contexts and her prior knowledge, Yutong used her first language as her linguistic resource. Although she used all language cueing systems, she relies more on the linguistics systems and less on the pragmatic systems.

Yutong had stronger comprehension when she effectively transacted with the image and made connections. When the text became more challenging to understand, Yutong used multiple strategies to support her construction of meaning. She reread the text, omitted unnecessary information, used different cueing systems, referred to the image for visual aid and connections, and related to prior knowledge and experience.

Yutong read both the texts and diagrams, focused more on the written texts than the diagrams, and understood the texts better when effectively interacting with the images and making connections. This result is also aligned with a study showing that English as a Foreign Language readers focus more on the written text than the visuals when they read science texts (Hung et al., 2019; Chapter 9). Although Yutong had prior knowledge about the first text, her retelling score was slightly higher for "Multimedia Learning." The reason could be that she made more integrative transitions in the second text and reported that she was selecting information from both the text and the image. This supports previous research that shows that students who made more transitions to the image comprehended the science texts better (Hung, 2014). Additionally, Yutong connected to her prior experience and used the theory introduced in "Multimedia Learning" to reflect on her field experience.

Implications

College English learners use the same reading process as that of native speakers. Regardless of the languages that the readers speak, reading is a meaning-making process. Teachers can help readers by conferring with them about their strategies and meaning making process. One possibility is for teachers to play the video clips we provide in this chapter and show the students that reading is not word-by-word or invite the students to discuss the EMMA focus questions, such as "What do you observe the reader doing?" and "How do your observations of this reader's reading influence your view of what reading is?" (Kim, Duckett, & Brown, 2010, p. 13).

Teachers can also guide students to use visual aids and connect to their prior knowledge or previous experiences for understanding; demonstrate how to read the figures, diagrams, tables, and graphs in the academic reading materials; and encourage students constantly to make connections to their readings particularly when they read challenging texts. When teachers work with students from linguistically diverse backgrounds, they should remember that students' dialects, accents, or other language variations should not affect their oral reading assessment. Teachers can help multilingual readers be strategic about how to approach text efficiently (Liwanag, Martens, Martens, & Pelatti, 2017). Further research could use EMMA and Retrospective EMMA (Paulson & Freeman, 2003) to study college students' reading process in different disciplines and students who speak different languages.

References

Arslan-Ari, I. (2013). *Examining the effects of cueing and prior knowledge on learning, mental effort, and study time in a complex animation* (Unpublished doctoral dissertation). Texas Tech University, Lubbock, TX.

Feathers, K., & Arya, P. (2015). Exploring young children's use of illustrations in a picture book. *Language and Literacy, 17*(1), 42–62.

Fennes, H., & Hapgood, K. (1997). *Intercultural learning in the classroom.* London & Washington: Cassell.

Flurkey, A. (2008). Reading flow. In A. Flurkey, E. Paulson, & K. Goodman (Eds.), *Scientific realism in studies of reading* (pp. 267–304). New York: Taylor & Francis Group.

Hung, Y. (2014). "What are you looking at?" An eye movement exploration in science text reading. *International Journal of Science and Mathematics Education, 12*(2), 241–260.

Hung, Y., Kuo, H., & Liao, S. (2019). Seeing what they see: Elementary EFL students reading science texts. *RELC Journal*, doi: 10.1177/0033688219854475

Goodman, K. (1994). Reading, writing, and written texts: A transactional sociopsycholinguistic view. In R. Ruddell, M. Ruddell, & H. Singer (Eds.), *Theoretical models and processes of reading* (4th ed., pp. 1093–1130). Newark, DE: International Reading Association.

Goodman, K. (1996). *On reading: A common-sense look at the nature of language and the science of reading.* Portsmouth, NH: Heinemann.

Goodman, Y., Watson, D., & Burke, C. (2005). *Reading miscue inventory.* NY: Richard C. Owen.

Institute of International Education. (2017). International student enrollment trends, 1948/49–2016/17. *Open Doors Report on International Educational Exchange.* Retrieved from http://www.iie.org/opendoors

Isakson, R., & Isakson, M. (2017). Preparing college students to learn more from academic texts through metacognitive awareness of reading strategies. In K. Mokhtari (Ed.), *Improving reading comprehension through metacognitive reading strategies instruction* (pp. 155–176). Lanham, MD: Rowman & Littlefield.

Johnson, C., & Mayer, R. (2012). An eye movement analysis of the spatial contiguity effect in multimedia learning. *Journal of Experimental Psychology, 18*(2), 178–191.

Kim, K., Duckett, P., & Brown, J. (2010). Reframing the reading process through EMMA. *Talking Points, 22*(1), 10–14.

Li, W. (1992). *Chinese and English reading miscues of six Chinese graduate students* (Unpublished doctoral dissertation). University of Missouri, Columbia, MO.

Liwanag, M. P. S. U., Martens, P., Martens, R. & Pelatti, C. Y. (2017). Supporting multilingual learners as readers: Lessons from Eye Movement and Miscue Analysis. *English Journal, 106*(3), 79–82.

Liwanag, M. P. S. U., Pelatti, C. Y., Martens, R., & Martens, P. (2016). Children's eye movements, miscue analysis patterns, and retellings when reading a counterpoint picture book. *Literacy Research: Theory, Method, and Practice, 65*(1), 253–267.

Mason, L., Scheiter, K., & Tornatora, M. C. (2017). Using eye movements to model the sequence of text–picture processing for multimedia comprehension. *Journal of Computer Assisted Learning, 33*(5), 443–460.

Mason, L., Tornatora, M. C., & Pluchino, P. (2013). Do fourth graders integrate text and picture in processing and learning from an illustrated science text? Evidence from eye-movement patterns. *Computers & Education, 60*(1), 95–09.

Mason, L., Tornatora, M. C., & Pluchino, P. (2015). Integrative processing of verbal and graphical information during re-reading predicts learning from illustrated text: An eye-movement study. *Reading and Writing, 28*(6), 851–872.

Mayer, R. (2009). *Multimedia learning* (2nd ed.). New York: Cambridge University Press.

McKenna, M., & Robinson, R. (2014). *Teaching through text: Reading and writing in the content areas.* Upper Saddle River, NJ: Pearson.

Moore, R., & Gilles, C. (2005). *Reading conversations: Retrospective miscue analysis with struggling readers, grades 4–12.* Portsmouth, NH: Heinemann.

Nist, S., & Simpson, M. (2000). College studying. In M. Kamil, P. Mosenthal, P. Pearson, & R. Barr (Eds.), *Handbook of reading research* (Vol. III, pp. 645–666). Mahwah, NJ: Erlbaum.

Paulson, E. (2000). *Adult readers' eye movements during the production of oral miscues.* (Unpublished doctoral dissertation). University of Arizona, Tucson, AZ.

Paulson, E., & Freeman, A. (2003). *Insight from the eyes: The science of effective reading instruction.* Portsmouth, NH: Heinemann.

Paulson, E., & Goodman, K. (2008). Re-reading eye-movement research: Support for transactional models of reading. In A. Flurkey, E. Paulson, & K. Goodman (Eds.), *Scientific realism in studies of reading* (pp. 25–47). New York: Lawrence Erlbaum Associates.

Rosenblatt, L. (1978). *The reader, the text, the poem.* Carbondale: Southern Illinois University Press.

Stake, R. (1995). *The art of case study research.* Thousand Oaks, CA: Sage.

Tobii Pro (2020, May 8). *Working with Heatmap and Gaze Plots.* Retrieved from https://www.tobiipro.com/learn-and-support/learn/steps-in-an-eye-tracking-study/interpret/working-with-heat-maps-and-gaze-plots/

Unsworth, L. (2004). Comparing school science explanations in books and computer-based format: The role of images, image/text relations and hyperlinks. *International Journal of Instructional Media, 31*(3), 283–301.

Wang, Y. (2014). *Reading in Mandarin and English: Using reading miscue inventory and retrospective miscue analysis with adult English language learners* (Unpublished dissertation). University of Missouri, Columbia, MO.

Wang, Y. (2019). Exploring meaningfulness: Perceptions and strategy use of Chinese international graduate students in disciplinary reading. *Journal of International Students, 9*(2), 661–681.

Wang, Y., & Gilles, C. (2017). Reading in English and in Chinese: Case study of Retrospective Miscue Analysis with two adult ELs. *Reading Horizons, 56*(2), 64–92.

Zhang, L., & Wu, A. (2009). Chinese senior high school EFL students' metacognitive awareness and reading-strategy use. *Reading in a Foreign Language, 21*(1), 37–59.

Eye Movement Recording Vignettes:

Arslan-Ari, I. (2020, August 7). *Sample eye movements for possible outcomes of interculture encounters* [Video file]. Retrieved from https://youtu.be/n1gl0hGkY7M

Arslan-Ari, I. (2019, February 21) *Miscue of not* [Video file]. Retrieved from https://youtu.be/c-I41Mg_U3w

Arslan-Ari, I. (2019, August 28) *Miscue culture* [Video file]. Retrieved from https://youtu.be/GpTAG2A1k2c

Arslan-Ari, I. (2019, February 21) *Integrative transitions* [Video file]. Retrieved from https://youtu.be/nHXyjbZN0v8

12

Exploring a University Learner's Disciplinary Literacies Using Eye Movement Miscue Analysis (EMMA)

by Heather D. Porter, Koomi J. Kim, and Judith K. Franzak

As college students pursue specialized areas of study, they are expected to engage in literacy practices specific to the academic domain of the field. Because the foundation of academic learning at the college level is literacy-based (Holschuh, 2019) in a broad sense, the perspective of disciplinary literacy is critical to understanding how reading and writing involve more than background knowledge of subject material. Effective engagement with subject-matter texts also requires a *disciplinary stance*—an awareness of the values embedded in the specialized ways a field creates and communicates knowledge (Porter, 2018).

Although researchers acknowledge the relationship between college literacy and learning outcomes (Holschuh & Paulson, 2013) and promote the need for specialized comprehension strategies (Hynd-Shanahan, 2013), a gap remains in research into how college readers negotiate and integrate their knowledge of literacy, content, and context (Porter, 2018). Using eye movement miscue analysis (EMMA), we explore the meaning-making processes of one upper-division college reader, Beth (pseudonym), whose experiences help us understand how stance mediates a reader's meaning making processes. Specifically, our inquiry is guided by the following question: What does EMMA data reveal about the nature of a college reader's disciplinary-specific meaning making processes (i.e., the content-specific knowledge and strategies employed) while reading an authentic text?

EMMA and Disciplinary Literacy

As other authors in this book describe, EMMA methods reflect a sociopsycholinguistic transactional reading model (Goodman & Goodman, 2013). In this model, readers are actively negotiating their understanding through their transactions with texts by drawing upon their background knowledge, sociolinguistic schema, and situated stances as they construct a parallel text representing their unique interpretation of meaning (Goodman, Fries, & Strauss, 2016). EMMA demonstrates reading through an integrated analysis of eye movements, documenting the perceptive activity of readers' visual processing of a text, and miscue analysis, revealing the knowledge and strategies readers draw upon to make sense of text as they read orally (Paulson, Flurkey, Goodman, & Goodman, 2003). While often used to understand young readers' processes, EMMA has been effective in supporting college readers' awareness of their strengths as readers and their conceptualizations of reading as a meaning-making process (Porter, Kim, Franzak, & MacDonald, 2020; Wang & Gilles, 2017).

In situating both text and reader within the context of academic domains, a disciplinary literacy perspective emphasizes the ideological influences on comprehending processes. These ways of thinking about and communicating knowledge are subsumed into the language and structure of texts (Geisler, 2004). Such discourse patterns implicitly necessitate the use of specialized knowledge and interpretative strategies as readers construct domain-specific meaning. Readers also enact disciplinary schema—mental models comprised of their background knowledge of content as well as dispositions and ways of thinking (Porter, 2018). Past expert-reader studies illustrate this phenomenon by describing how the purposes behind readers' strategy use influences their comprehending processes (Fang, 2012). For example, to understand the significance underlying historians' strategy to corroborate sources while reading requires an awareness of how historical argumentation informs and mediates such an approach to reading historical texts.

Process of EMMA Inquiry

This EMMA inquiry was designed as an exploratory case study of one college student's experience reading an authentic text (Hesse-Biber, 2017). Data were collected from two sessions over the duration of one year. In order to gain an understanding of Beth's self-perceptions of the purpose and processes involved in reading, we facilitated a 65-minute discussion with her using the Burke Reading Interview Modified for Older Readers (Goodman, Watson, Burke, 2005). Beth then participated in an EMMA session, lasting about 60 minutes, where she read aloud a 601-word sample from a translated text, entitled "The Four Great Errors," excerpted from the German philosopher Friedrich Nietzsche's (n.d.) *Twilight of the Idols*. Beth selected this reading based on her personal interests and prior recommendation of her philosophy adviser.

Although she had not read this text prior to this EMMA session, she was familiar with this German philosopher's larger body of work and recognized it as an upcoming assigned course reading. Having participated in an EMMA session in a related study conducted by the research team, Beth was familiar with the eye-tracking device and methods and understood the non-evaluative intent of recording her natural reading process.

During the EMMA session we collected oral reading samples in addition to eye movement and miscue data using a SR Research (2017) desktop eye tracker, EyeLink 1000 PLUS and Data Viewer software, which calculated her eye movements in relation to the screen text. After the oral reading was completed, we facilitated and recorded a debriefing session, including unaided and aided retellings, where Beth reflected on her understanding of the text in order to observe and document the extent of her comprehension in relation to the miscue data collected (Goodman et al., 2016).

Data analysis was a recursive and iterative process that followed standard EMMA procedures. The initial cycle of coding focused on marking Beth's miscues as she read the text aloud using the reading miscue inventory (RMI) Classroom Procedure to document her miscues and her reading strategies (Goodman et al., 2005). Second cycle analysis involved coding the miscues with the eye movement data produced from the Data Viewer software's video recording of Beth as she read the text aloud, which included a visual representation of her eye fixations and saccades in addition to the actual video recording of her eye movements. A final cycle of analysis involved triangulating the corpus of coded miscue data with Beth's unaided and aided retellings of the texts in which she recounted her comprehension of the text and her use of comprehending strategies as she read. Through the triangulation of multiple data sources and analytic cycles, this single case study offers a rich, thick description of this college reader's comprehending and comprehension processes substantiated by multiple, authentic accounts of her reading (Hesse-Biber, 2017).

Beth

Beth is a monolingual white female who, at the time of this study, was 21 years old and enrolled in her senior year at a comprehensive public university in the mid-Atlantic region pursuing a double major in philosophy and psychology. Despite her academic success, evidenced by her 3.9 cumulative GPA, Beth described having to learn "to be patient" with herself as she developed her capacity to read and study philosophy. Beth shared how she developed her knowledge and strategies through a formal apprenticeship process facilitated by her undergraduate program that included a sophomore proseminar on reading and philosophical ways of thinking as well as course-specific instruction and a program-sponsored reading club. On her own, Beth immersed herself in experiences reading independently and participating in faculty-led discussions. Reflecting on her early experiences in the proseminar class, Beth described feeling impatient with the difficulty of reading Aristotle for the first time: "I thought there was no way I can ever get better at this, like everyone's telling me I just need to practice, and I was like 'but that doesn't help me get it now.'" She acknowledged her self-efficacy for philosophy reading has been challenging, stating, "I had to learn to be okay with how I read because if I'm always focusing on like, 'Oh you're not doing this right,' which happens a lot, then . . . that's all I start thinking about and I'm not getting anything out of it." Beth identifies herself as a "slow" and "thoughtful" reader, agreeing with her professor, who characterized her as "careful" in her reading process.

When asked to describe how she reads philosophy texts, Beth first acknowledged it can be an "overwhelming" activity because of the difficulties encountered with the genre's antiquated vocabulary, structural composition, and linguistic translations. She explained, "They [philosophers] talk in really complicated sentences . . . and they use language, like back in the old days . . . and words that don't fit the perfect English translation." Recognizing this as "something you got to get used to," she then offered several strategies that she had learned through her coursework for support. Prior to reading a text, Beth emphasized the importance of situating the philosopher in "the context of when they were writing" and to set the purpose for reading as understanding the philosopher's attempt to "establish some sort of truth" through argumentation, a central aspect of a philosopher's stance (Concepción, 2004).

She explained that while reading "it helps to look for those parts [the thesis, the argument, and counterpoints], because you can easily get lost . . . if there's no purpose to what you're doing." Beth reflected the need to read closely, defining the vocabulary in the context of the philosopher's time period and segmenting and re-reading sentences to interrogate and confirm her understanding. She further emphasized the importance of engaging herself in dialogue with the text, often reading aloud and pausing in order to make interpretive inferences about the text in light of her own conceptions, a process that supports her ability to think "deeply and critically" about larger philosophical ideas. Collectively, Beth's reflections about herself as a reader and her reading processes revealed her sense of emergent membership within her academic community as she expressed a keen awareness for how her meaning-making practices supported her disciplinary engagement and knowledge development.

EMMA Insights From Beth's Reading

The analysis of Beth's EMMA session offers insights into the situated nature of her reading processes driven by her enactment of stance and integration of reading strategies. In general, the results from the RMI and retelling data, as shown in Table 12.1, demonstrate her strengths as a constructive and highly proficient adult reader. The eye movement data revealed that Beth had 774 fixations as she read the 601-word text, indicating that she continuously sampled and re-sampled the text as she read. Her eye movement patterns revealed regressions occurring at points in the text with complex terminologies and lexico-grammar, which confirmed her active monitoring of her understanding of content and rhetorical moves (Porter et al., 2020). While past research indicates the mean duration of an adult reader's fixation is about 225–250 milliseconds during oral readings (Rayner & Castelhano, 2007), Beth's fixation duration averaged 303.43 milliseconds, suggesting that the flow of her reading was slightly longer than that of general reading (Flurkey, 2008). Additionally, the analysis of her comprehending processes indicates the efficacy of her reading strategies despite making twelve miscues as she read. Of the twelve miscues, Beth self-corrected two, and left the other ten uncorrected, seven of which resulted in no meaning change and the other three resulted in a partial change of meaning. Her miscues are considered high quality in that her ability to comprehend the text was minimally impacted, with a 10% partial strength (YYP). The YYP shows the semantic and syntactic acceptability (YY=Yes Yes) and partial meaning change (P=Partial). Collectively, these results indicate the

Title	The Four Great Errors
Text Word Count	601
Reading Duration	459.65s
Total Fixations	774
Mean Fixation Duration	303.43ms
Total Miscues	12
Miscues per Hundred Words (MPHW)	1.99
Comprehending Analysis	
Strength (YYN)	90%
Partial Strength (YYP)	10%
Meaning Loss (YYY;YN_;NN_)	0%
Retelling Holistic Score	Excellent

Table 12.1: Beth's Eye Movement and RMI Scores

Source: Authors.

strategies Beth employed to make sense of the text as she read were effective and efficient in supporting her understanding of the text, as further evidenced by the excellent holistic retelling score, which reflects her in-depth account of the text she read (Goodman et al., 2005). For example, during the retelling Beth described Nietzsche's argument and reflected on specific structural elements that were used to advance his position. In the discussion that follows, we explore these strategies in relation to what they reveal about her meaning-making processes.

Schema Driven Miscue

In this first example of Beth's reading, we focus our attention to exploring one of her high-quality miscues. Figure 12.1 shows Beth's eye movements as she made multiple miscues involving a substitution and then a partial self-correction:

> *Original text:* his friends say: that is because of this or that disease.

> *Beth's reading:* his *friend says*: that is because of *this is that [uh] that is because of this or that* disease.

Instead of reading the first part of the phrase in its original plural form, *his friends say*, Beth substituted the singular form, *his friend says*, without any pause or regression to confirm her prediction. As shown in Figure 12.1, fixation points 1-3 reveal she did not fixate on *say* as she read, illuminating how she efficiently integrated her knowledge of syntactic and semantic cues to infer and predict with a minimal disruption to meaning. At the same time, her eye movements indicated a regression during the second miscue of this sentence

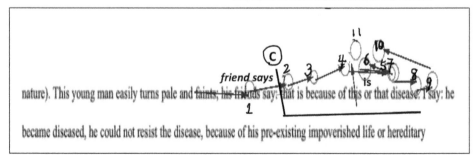

Figure 12.1: Beth's Eye Movements During a High-Quality Miscue

Source: Authors.
Source: Nietzsche, F. (n.d.). *Twilight of the idols*. Retrieved from
http://www.handprint.com/SC/NIE/GotDamer.html#sect6 (Original work published 1889)

when Beth initially read *that is because of this is that* instead of *that is because of this or that* (fixation numbers 4–7). In disconfirming her initial prediction (*this is that*), Beth paused and uttered "uh" as she regressed to self-correct (fixation numbers 7–11).

Taken together, these examples demonstrate Beth's strategic monitoring of her comprehension by drawing upon her schema of text structure. Although she did not self-correct her initial miscue (*his friend says*), she made a semantically and syntactically acceptable substitutions in her attempt to make sense of the text. She selectively sampled and regressed in the text for important ideas that were essential for her to confirm her understanding of the philosopher's argument. When asked about her approach to reading this text during the retelling session, Beth described how "good" philosophy texts incorporate metaphors and examples that embed philosophical reasoning to illustrate the thesis of the work, a structural feature of the text that Beth attended to more closely in order to "understand what it is doing for the [philosopher's] argument." In this excerpt of Beth's reading, she is making a schema-driven miscue by drawing upon her knowledge of philosophers' rhetorical moves in order to self-correct her initial reading and preserve the nuanced inference of the phrase.

Transforming Syntax

In a second example, Beth drew upon her semantic and syntactic knowledge to predict and transform syntax as an intentional scaffold to her meaning-making processes. Figure 12.2 demonstrates Beth's eye movements as she substituted a period for the semicolon included in the original text (fixation points 16–19):

> *Original text:* Every mortality, every religion, is based on this imperative; I call it the original sin of reason, the immortal unreason. In my mouth, this formula is changed into its opposite—the first example of my "revaluation of all values."

> *Beth's reading:* Every mortality, every religion, is based on this imperative*[.]* I call it the original sin of reason, *[inaudible]* the immortal unreason. In my mouth, this formula is changed into its opposite—the first example of my "revaluation of all values." *[Can I read that again?]*

Fixation point 18 demonstrates that Beth fixated on the semicolon before moving on to read the sentence, spending 350 milliseconds on this punctuation-related miscue, compared to her average fixation duration of 303.43 milliseconds across the text. The recording of her oral reading further confirmed Beth's period substitution as her intonation shifted and slowed as she substituted a period [.] for the semicolon [;].

As Beth continued to read, she further drew upon her substitution miscue to navigate her re-sampling strategies. After Beth read the phrase *the first*

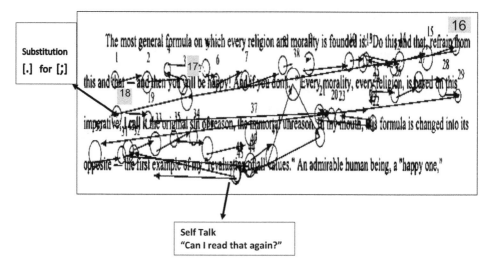

Figure 12.2: Beth's Eye Movements During Substitution Miscue of Period (Fixation Points 16–19) and Dynamic Re-sampling.

Source: Authors.

Source: Nietzsche, F. (n.d.). *Twilight of the idols*. Retrieved from http://www.handprint.com/SC/NIE/GotDamer.html#sect6 (Original work published 1889)

example of my "reevaluation of all values," she paused and asked to re-read starting from her substitution miscue of the period to read the content again, uttering an inaudible reaction after re-reading *I call it the original sin of reason.* During the retelling session Beth spoke of the importance of pausing and needing to re-read sentences multiple times in order to "soak it all up." Attributing the need for this strategy to both the amount and complexity of ideas contained in any one sentence, Beth suggested that by pausing she is better able to see how the philosopher's argument "unfolds for itself" as she described the need to consider how prior ideas shape and inform a text's ongoing argument.

Evidenced in Beth's description of her strategies is how she self-monitors her own reading processes to strategically navigate the syntactic structure of the text. Moreover, in this case her patterns of fixations on punctuation mirror the extent to which she fixated on content words throughout the text suggesting the significance of sentence structure as complementary to content for reading. While research indicates readers fixate more on content words than function words (Carpenter & Just, 1983), Beth demonstrated that punctuation fixations may also reveal important insights about reading. Specifically, the examples from Beth illustrate how she drew upon her syntactic and lexico-grammatical knowledge to transform complex text structures into manageable components as she constructed meaning across the whole of the text. For Beth, this strategy enabled her to put multiple ideas into conversation with one another in an effort to read more dialogically across the text, another key component of philosophy's stance (Concepción, 2004).

Transacting Through Disciplinary Stance

In this final excerpt of Beth's reading, we see how she actively engaged sampling and regressing strategies as she navigated the text (see Figure 12.3). Her regressions reveal how she drew upon the whole passage as she transacted meaning and selectively scanned the text in a non-linear manner. While Beth read the first portion of this text aloud in a serial manner, her eye movements demonstrate that she sampled frequently and recursively to effectively predict and confirm her inferences as she read the text aloud. As the Figure 12.3 shows, she did not fixate on every word, fixating more frequently on content words than function words, yet her awareness and integration of the language cueing systems (semantic, syntactic, and graphophonic cueing systems) allowed her to effectively construct meaning of the text.

In addition, her regressions indicate her strategies as a constructively responsive reader to address challenging areas she encountered in the text. The larger fixation points at the end of the example indicate Beth's longer fixation

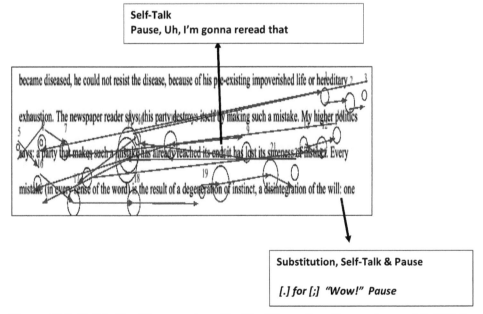

Figure 12.3: Beth's Eye Movements as She Used Sampling, Regressing, and Self-Talk Strategies

Source: Authors.
Source: Nietzsche, F. (n.d.). *Twilight of the idols.* Retrieved from
http://www.handprint.com/SC/NIE/GotDamer.html#sect6 (Original work published 1889)

durations as she adjusted the pace of her reading. Reflecting on her dynamic eye movements, Beth described that the semantic complexity language philosophers use to construct their arguments is difficult to process as a novice reader. She has learned that philosophers build their arguments through examples and metaphors, so, as a reader, she strategically allocates more time to those areas of the text as they provide the most useful information to interpret the thesis. In tandem with this strategy, Beth also described the importance of adopting a metacognitive process, informed by her developing disciplinary schema, to reflect and monitor her interpretative understanding of the text. She stated:

> You'll have that moment where . . . you literally . . . like to yourself you're like, "Ohh, that!" You just are like, "Oh, I get it," and other things will fall into place . . . because like once you get that you'll be like, "Oh, so that's why this is like this," and once you can start doing that then you're like "all right, I got something."

Across her reading of this text, Beth paused and uttered self-talk as she negotiated meaning at nine distinct points. Fixation points 8–10 and 19–22 in Figure 12.3 depict two of these instances where Beth verbalized her reactions and paused while her eyes scanned across the text:

> *Original text:* My higher politics says: a party that makes such a mistake has already reached its end; it has lost its sureness of instinct. Every mistake (in every sense of the word) is the result of a degree of degeneration of instinct, a disintegration of the will: one...

> *Beth's reading:* My higher politics says: a party that makes such a mistake has already reached its end; *[Pause] [Uh, I'm gonna reread that.]* a party that makes such a mistake has already reached its end; *it's* lost its sureness of instinct. Every mistake (in every sense of the word) is *a* result of degeneration of instinct, a disintegration of the will *[.] [Wow!] [Pause]*

When asked about why she made those comments, Beth explained, "The end like, the end just kind of blew me away," alluding to the impact of Nietzsche's argument. As a reading strategy, Beth emphasized the necessity of reading texts as an interpretive process aimed at informing the reader's ability to make logical and critical inferences and interpretations about philosophical ideas:

> I read for meaning . . . philosophy has to be a lived thing. You don't get philosophy by reading [texts], you read and then you think . . . then if I have that dialogue [alluding to dialogue with the philosophers], then I'll come out of the truth. In essence, they [the philosophers] try to get you to think about things in a way that you never thought before.

The oral and EMMA data of Beth's reading reveal how she embodied this stance as she transacted with this text, inserting thoughtful dialogic reactions into the text as she processed her understanding.

In terms of reading processes, Beth's eye movements offer insights into the continuous perceptual activity (Goodman et al., 2016) she engaged as she read this philosophy text. The examples, coupled with her reflective understanding, illustrate Beth's effectiveness as a strategic reader who integrates her awareness of stance with her reading strategies to construct a meaningful understanding of the text in alignment with philosophy's values and traditions.

Reflections on Inquiry

The EMMA analysis of Beth's reading offers important insights into the dynamic and complex enactment of disciplinary literacy by illuminating the importance of stance. Evidenced across the findings is Beth's developing sociocognitive awareness of philosophy in terms of how she drew upon her background knowledge of content as well as her understanding of the particular ways of thinking about and communicating knowledge valued by this domain. Although this inquiry captures only one novice's experience reading in philosophy, Beth's reading offers an authentic account of her mediation of stance through her meaning-making processes and prompts new insights into how we understand, explore, and teach literacy across content areas.

In terms of stance, Beth's reading reveals new ways of understanding how domain-specific meaning-making lenses are simultaneously developing and enacted by novice readers. As Beth navigated this text, she read dialogically, as opposed to in a linear manner, revealing how she made intertextual connections within the text and to her prior knowledge. Throughout this process, she made several schema-driven miscues illustrating how she was navigating both stance and text simultaneously. She navigated language structures and syntax to situate her understanding within the paradigm of logical argumentation as would be expected from philosophy's stance. This analysis illustrates how Beth was reading beyond the text to make domain-specific interpretations of the function and purpose of the author's rhetorical moves in light of her understanding of philosophy's practice of engaging in and evaluating arguments.

In light of these findings, we wonder about the potential for new lines of inquiry regarding disciplinary literacy. As Beth drew upon punctuation and rhetorical conventions to navigate her pace and flow of reading, we are curious about the role of punctuation and syntax to communicate specialized ways of thinking. While Beth's reading highlights how philosophy invokes logical reasoning through metaphors and examples, how does punctuation serve to mediate such embedded meanings? Furthermore, as Beth's reading was a translated text, how do philosophers interpret whether particular writing choices are authorial intentions or interpretations made by the translator? While we recognize this as part of stance, our findings suggest potential for future studies that would benefit from using EMMA as a method of inquiry.

In terms of supporting novice readers' development of these specialized literacy practices, students need immersive experiences with authentic texts—that include exposure as well as instruction—in order to build their endurance for reading independently and agency for academic engagement (Holschuh, 2019; Porter, 2018). Although building background knowledge of content is important, students also need to understand and connect strategies with purpose. All teachers of college and adolescent readers should scaffold students' development of disciplinary stance including specific metacognitive awareness for reading strategies and meaning-making processes just as Beth experienced throughout her college reading apprenticeship. In doing this work, instructors should teach students to read beyond the text, to understand the role of syntax and language structures in shaping a text's message, as a critical component in preparing novices for deep, dialogic transactions with texts.

Despite the acknowledgment that college reading involves higher-level literacy knowledge and strategies, some postsecondary learners carry misconceptions about the purpose and nature of reading as a meaning-making process as well as their own self-efficacy as meaning makers (Porter et al., 2020). Yet Beth shows us reading is a dynamic, constructive process that is not solely a text-based activity, but a domain-specific, participatory process that requires a dialogical engagement between readers, texts, and their larger academic domains. Her EMMA analysis offers powerful insights into the strategies and ways of thinking she used to engage in the authentic work of philosophy as an emerging member of the discipline.

References

Carpenter P., & Just, M. A. (1983). What your eyes do while your mind is reading. In K. Rayner (Ed.), *Eye movements in reading: Perceptual and language processes* (pp. 275–307). New York: Academic Press.

Concepción, D. W. (2004). Reading philosophy with background knowledge and metacognition. *Teaching Philosophy, 27*(4), 351–368.

Fang, Z. (2012). Language correlates of disciplinary literacy. *Topics in Language Disorders, 32*(1), 19–34.

Flurkey, A. (2008). Reading flow. In K. Goodman, E. Paulson, & A. Flurkey (Eds.), *Scientific realism in studies of reading* (pp. 267–304). Mahwah, NJ: Laurence Erlbaum.

Geisler, C. 2004. *Academic literacy and the nature of expertise: Reading, writing and knowing in academic philosophy.* Hillsdale, NJ: Lawrence Erlbaum.

Goodman, K., Fries, P. H., & Strauss, S. L. (2016). *Reading, the grand illusion: How and why people make sense of print.* New York: Routledge.

Goodman, Y.M., & Goodman, K.S. (2013). To err is human: Learning about language processes by analyzing miscues. In D. Alvermann, N. Unrau, & R. Ruddell (Eds.), *Theoretical models and processes of reading*, (6th ed., pp. 525–543). Newark, DE: International Reading Association.

Goodman, Y., Watson, D., & Burke, C. (2005). *Reading miscue inventory*. Katonah, NY: Richard Owen Publishers.

Hesse-Biber, S. N. (2017). *The practice of qualitative research* (3rd ed.). Thousand Oaks, CA: Sage.

Holschuh, J. P. (2019). College reading and studying: The complexity of academic literacy demands. *Journal of Adolescent & Adult Literacy, 62*(6), 599–604.

Holschuh, J. P., & Paulson, E. J. (2013, July). *The terrain of college developmental reading* [White paper]. Retrieved from College Reading and Learning Association: http://207.250.94.50/images/whitepaper/TheTerrainofCollege91913.pdf

Hynd-Shanahan, C. (2013). What does it take? The challenge of disciplinary literacy. *Journal of Adolescent & Adult Literacy, 57*(2), 93–98.

Nietzsche, F. (n.d.). *Twilight of the idols*. Retrieved from http://www.handprint.com/SC/NIE/GotDamer.html#sect6 (Original work published 1889)

Paulson, E., Flurkey, A., Goodman, Y., & Goodman, K. (2003). Eye movements and miscue analysis: Reading from a constructivist perspective. *The fifty-second yearbook of the National Reading Conference, 52*, 343–355.

Porter, H. (2018). *Co-constructing undergraduate disciplinary literacy: A case study of disciplinary communities* (Unpublished dissertation). Salisbury University, Salisbury.

Porter, H., Kim, K., Franzak, J., & MacDonald, K. (2020). Reframing and repositioning college readers' assumptions about reading through eye movement miscue analysis. *Journal of Adolescent & Adult Literacy, 63*(5), 519–528.

Rayner, K., & Castelhano, M. (2007). Eye movements. *Scholarpedia, 2*(10): 3649. doi: 10.4249/scholarpedia.3649

SR Research (2017). *EyeLink 1000 plus user manual*. Version 1.0.9. Ontario, Canada.

Wang, Y., & Gilles, C. J. (2017). Reading in English and in Chinese: Case study of retrospective miscue analysis with two adult English learners. *Reading Horizons, 56*(2), 64–92.

Contributing Author Biographies

Laura E. Arrington is an Assistant Professor in Communicative Disorders at the University of Louisiana at Lafayette. She has worked as a speech-language pathologist for over 15 years in a variety of settings. Her primary areas of interest are literacy, language disorders, mild traumatic brain injury, and qualitative research methodology.

Poonam Arya is a Professor of Reading, Language, and Literature at Wayne State University. Her research interests include studying collaborative discussions of videos to support teachers' reflective practice and decision-making processes; and eye movements, retellings, and oral readings of children as they transact with multimodal texts. Her work has appeared in journals such as Reading Research Quarterly and Language Arts.

Ismahan Arslan-Ari is an Assistant Professor in the Educational Technology program at the University of South Carolina. She received her doctorate in Instructional Technology with a minor in Special Education (Deafblind) from Texas Tech University. Her research mainly focuses on multimedia learning, human computer interaction, the use of assistive technologies, and web-based learning systems.

Charlotte Clark is an Assistant Professor of Communicative Disorders at the University of Wisconsin, Eau Claire. Her research interests include child language and literacy and language disorders.

Holly L. Damico is an Associate Professor of Communicative Disorders at the University of Louisiana at Lafayette and Co-director of the Language and

Literacy Project. Her research involves language and literacy acquisition and disorders, qualitative research methods, and apprenticeship models of learning.

Jack S. Damico is a Professor of Communicative Disorders at University of Colorado, Boulder. He was Doris B. Hawthorne Eminent Scholar in Special Education and Communicative Disorders for 28 years at the University of Louisiana, Lafayette. He's published widely in qualitative research methodologies in persons with communication and literacy impairments.

Meghan East is an Instructor at Salisbury University in the Department of Health Sciences, and also works a physician assistant in private practice. She is currently a doctoral student in the Department of Literacy Studies. Her research interests are in disciplinary literacy in the adult learner and emergent literacy practices in young children. She is interested in EMMA, adult literacies, and critical literacies.

Karen M. Feathers is known internationally for her work in content reading, comprehension, and staff development. She has published in a variety of sources, and her book Infotext: Reading and Learning has been translated and used internationally. She has been actively engaged in professional organizations and is now retired from Wayne State University. She continues with her research and teaching through local institutions and organizations.

D. Jake Follmer is an educational psychologist. His research focuses on the roles of cognitive and metacognitive skills in learning and strategy use. He is particularly interested in interdisciplinary research that examines how learners' regulatory skills support comprehension of expository text. He has worked on several research projects, funded by the National Science Foundation and Psi Chi.

Judith K. Franzak is a Professor in the Department of Literacy Studies at Salisbury University. She is a former middle school and high school English teacher. Her research addresses questions of pedagogy and policy with a particular focus on adolescent literacy learners. Her publications include articles in English Education, The Teaching of Research in English, The Journal of Adolescent and Adult Literacy, and Children's Literature in Education.

Kenneth S. Goodman (1927–2020) was Professor Emeritus at the University of Arizona. He was the founding father of whole language. His seminal work includes the development of miscue analysis to study reading as a meaning-making process. He has published numerous books and articles. His work on miscue analysis and eye movement miscue analysis is included in Reading, the Grand Illusion: How and Why People Make Sense of Print.

Yueh-Nu Hung is an Associate Professor of the Department of English at National Taichung University of Education, Taiwan. Her main research interests are the cognitive processes, learning, and teaching of English and Chinese reading. Her recent research focuses on using the eye movement miscue analysis (EMMA) research method to understand reading processes of various text genres and types.

Lisa Kervin is a Professor and Researcher in Language and Literacy at the University of Wollongong, Australia, where she leads the Play, Curriculum and Pedagogy Early Start Research group. Lisa is Associate Dean of Research for the Faculty of Arts, Humanities and Social Sciences. Lisa's research interests include: (1) children's literacy practices; (2) children' use and understanding of technology and digital literacies; (3) and supporting teachers' use of technology.

Koomi J. Kim is a Professor at Salisbury University in the Department of Literacy Studies. Her areas of specialization include literacy education, multimodal, multiple and multilingual literacies, EMMA (Eye Movement and Miscue Analysis), RMA (Retrospective Miscue Analysis) and critical literacies.

Maria Perpetua Socorro U. Liwanag is an Associate Professor in the Department of Elementary Education at Towson University. Her research interests include eye movement miscue analysis (EMMA), literacy assessments, children's literature, critical and digital literacies. Her work has been published in Literacy Research: Theory, Method and Practice, English Journal, Childhood Education Journal, and Talking Points.

Jessica Mantei is Associate Professor in Language and Literacy and Head of Teaching and Learning in the School of Education at the University of Wollongong, Australia. Jessica is a member of the Play, Curriculum and Pedagogy in Early Start Research Group. Jessica's research interests include pedagogies for literacy teaching supported by technology; teacher reflective capacities and professional identity; and young children as consumers and producers of text.

Prisca Martens is Professor Emerita at Towson University. In addition to eye movement, her research and writing interests include early literacy, picturebooks, miscue analysis, and retrospective miscue analysis.

Honor B. McElroy is a doctoral student and graduate research assistant in the Department of Literacy Studies at Salisbury University. In addition to adolescent writing in out-of-school contexts, Honor is interested in the insights EMMA can provide about adolescent and adult readers.

Ryan L. Nelson is Department Head of Communicative Disorders at the University of Louisiana at Lafayette. His research interests include language and literacy development in childhood with language disorders and wellness approaches to counseling in communicative disorders. He has published in EMMA, counseling, and social-pragmatic approaches to autism.

Amanda Percle is completing a doctoral degree in Applied Speech and Language Sciences at the University of Louisiana at Lafayette. She has worked in public schools as a speech-language pathologist. Her interests include literacy, language disorders in children, eye-movement analysis, and qualitative research methodology.

Heather D. Porter is an Assistant Professor in the Department of Literacy Studies at Salisbury University. Her current research focuses on college and adult literacy development with emphases on disciplinary literacy and students' participatory trajectories within and beyond college learning contexts. Her work has been published in journals such as Journal of College Reading and Learning and Journal of Adolescent & Adult Literacy.

Shannon Tucker is the Assistant Dean of Instructional Design and Technology at the University of Maryland School of Pharmacy in Baltimore, MD and a doctoral student in Instructional Technology at Towson University. Shannon's current research interests include multimedia learning, design and user experience, information processing, and eye tracking.

Yang Wang is an Associate Professor in Language and Literacy in the Department of Instruction and Teacher Education at The University of South Carolina, Columbia. Her areas of interest are reading comprehension, reading assessment, English language teaching and learning, multicultural literatures, and global literatures.

Christine Weill is the Director of the Speech, Language, and Hearing Center at the University of Louisiana at Lafayette. Her clinical and research interests include: Autism Spectrum Disorders, language and literacy, and literacy development and social interaction.

CPSIA information can be obtained
at www.ICGtesting.com
Printed in the USA
BVHW041915020222
627903BV00007B/73